FAMILY RITUALS . . .

As a contemporary twist on Sabbath rest, we have high tea on Sunday evenings. Certain plates and platters come out just for this event. They are nothing more than thrift shop finds, but once they hit the table, they become heroic, met with expectation and excitement. We light candles, sing, and nibble on treats. In the early days, our treat used to be popcorn. We've graduated to Swiss chocolate and sweet pear sandwiches—an invention of my son's. Come measles or tax time, we still relish our tea together.

FAMILY SPIRITUALITY . . .

This is an especially hard concept to claim. In our age of diversity and individuality it is hard to find a common definition. We know only that we need it. For some it's formal worship, for others it is an evening meal indulged in, oblivious of time. Spirituality is profoundly connected to discovering meaning, and if we can understand how to activate meaning, we begin to get at our own spiritual life. Discovering, creating, and assigning meaning to the everyday nourishes this kind of timeless spirituality.

HOME LIFE . . .

My mother has an old sauce pot whose lid never quite fits. In one and only one position would that silly lid not tip and fall into boiling water. Home for a visit, I rummaged through the cabinet, determined to toss it out and get her one that wouldn't scald her. When my mother discovered my purpose, she calmly pulled out the pot and the lid and pointed to an arrow painted on each of them. "Before your father died, he painted these to show me where the lid fits. Don't ever throw this out." There it is. That place, that pot, where the two arrows meet—that's home.

The
Art
of
Family

Rituals, Imagination, and
Everyday Spirituality

❧

Gina Bria

A Dell Trade Paperback

A DELL TRADE PAPERBACK

Published by
Dell Publishing
a division of
Bantam Doubleday Dell Publishing Group, Inc.
1540 Broadway
New York, New York 10036

Copyright © 1998 by Gina Bria

Book design by Susan Maksuta

Library of Congress Cataloging in Publication Data
Bria, Gina.
The art of family : rituals, imagination, and everyday spirituality /
Gina Bria.
p.   cm.
ISBN 0-440-50772-3
1. Family—United States.   2. Family—Religious aspects—
Christianity.   I. Title.
HQ535.B75   1998
306.85—dc21   97-39217
CIP

Printed in the United States of America

Published simultaneously in Canada

June 1998

10   9   8   7   6   5   4   3   2   1

BVG

To my ever-widening family, the one I was rooted in and the one I made; and at the spinning core, to James.

I take pleasure in giving acknowledgment to Mary Ellen O'Neill, my editor at Dell Publishing, who brought this book to life.

PREFACE

A family is a kind of cup, into which we pour ourselves. As an anthropologist, I love studying ritual and kinship and the crazy habits of people near and far, so raising a family is, for me, a special commingling of work and life. In that, I am privileged, sort of like a chef who gets to try out unusual recipes at home. Margaret Mead is my Julia Child, an in-house, interior voice always standing at my elbow saying, "Now, can you explain to me why are you doing it *that* way?" I admit it, I've been doing an ethnography of my own family, what else could I do among the banal tasks of homelife? "What," I've asked myself, "are the central elements of family life that cannot be left behind?" Do we know anymore? What does it take to make a family last? What keeps us together? The notion of a shared culture naturally leapt to mind—that's how anthropologists explain everything. But it is true that working together, playing together, sharing rituals and spirituality, having a sense of living environment, and caring for one another's physical needs, are all the sure and ancient markers of an incorporated, living culture. And this is what families are—little societies.

While we are theoretically stuck with family members from birth until death, families do not naturally last a lifetime. Anything beyond simple biological affiliation must be created—all in a day's work. The high achievement is to make a family, a little society, that sustains its members through each of their lives. Success at this takes support from many sources, and I hope this book will be a source: for parents, old or new, grandparents, stepfamilies, families kept apart by distance; put upon by our own crazy culture.

As Thomas Moore notes in *Care of the Soul: Cultivating Depth and Sacredness in Everyday Life,* the fundamental problem with the family is one of imagination. I thoroughly agree, but how do we apply imagination to family? Once we think of families as a cultural creation, up there with all great cultural acts of art and history, we can begin to construct families from our own circumstances, whole or broken. But for this we need to be inspired by stories and reminded by vivid illustrations. I bear fresh water from old sources: play, ritual, imagination, story. Alchemy happens when they are reinjected into contemporary family life. Herein are family voices describing the sustaining power of the daily life of family, the spiritual life of family, the physical life of family, each with its own rituals, language, and place, alerting us to how we can forge lasting families for ourselves. Imagination, memories, and rituals are always at work in family lives, but perhaps unawares. We, like people everywhere, often instinctively practice many of these concepts. The trick is consciously claiming their inherent binding power and amplifying the positive effect in today's culture.

Like it or not, we are reinventing families with new forms, new roles, new expectations, but we are also failing at it at astronomical rates. This is a harsh environment to build a family in. How do we make our families last when so many lie broken around us? After experiencing a torn family ourselves, how do we find courage to go on? How do we make a family out of isolated lives? We want joy and endurance in our relationships, because relationships are the most exciting thing that can happen to us. Certainly this is not a guide or manual to "achieving" family. Instead, it is a book about applied hope and intelligence, a short definition of imagination, on the topic of living in families for a lifetime. It is about the resilience of relationships and identity in family through our lifetime. The stories and ideas here offer a long-range vision from which to draw strength and promise—an intended shout of encouragement. I hope it will convince readers that families are created, not inherited, and created among the lasting things in the grasp of the everyday.

This book is a result, and a gift, of imaginative families and friendships. You will spot yourself and your friends in the stories easily. Most of all, I hope this book and its stories will be a new imaginative friend to you, sparking new ideas, offering solace, giving rest.

And because I hope it to be a kind and steady friend, too, it's written to be laid down and picked up whenever you need it.

One

Creating a Family That Lasts a Lifetime

THE PLACE OF ONE'S OWN

*O*nce I took my children to a museum—one in a stroller, the other in a backpack. It was an empty day. We walked very close to the paintings. I bent and lifted one child out of the stroller, all the way up, face-to-face, with a portrait, while the child in the backpack peered over. "Look," I whispered to them, "look at the eyes. And the color of that hair. See those beautiful robes?" When I turned around, I discovered an audience—a few stray patrons and a guard—inching closer to hear what I could possibly have to say to the under-two crowd. But it wasn't an art lesson. I was giving myself to my children. Paintings mean a great deal to me and I wanted them to know why. I wanted them to know my loves, my reactions, my reasons, because even before they could speak, I wanted to speak to them. I wanted to be seen by my own children, to make them want me my whole life.

Only motherhood stood in my way, a concept high and loaded.

Long before I got out the door with my first diaper bag, I already knew I was operating on different principles of motherhood than the culture around me, not high culture like art and music, but the everyday operating culture. I live in an age that no longer believes in the absolute thrill of the individual, one premised on grace. No, I occupy an achievement culture, an adequacy culture, not one that forgives and enjoys, but one that performs, criticizes, and demands; one that prizes what we do, not what we are. Not that I didn't want my children to be prizes too. I wanted them to be finely educated, well spoken, possibly wise. But I wanted them to be more than products I had successfully turned out on the motherhood assembly line. I wanted them to be creatures who loved me, not only for what I did for them, but because of who I am—in all facets of my life, whether directly relevant to my children or not. I did not want my children to love me because I had been an adequate mother, because I would never be one, this I already knew. I wanted my children to love me for the same reason I want my children themselves to be loved: because we are all irreducible, irreplaceable.

In our landscape of anxiety, we are haunted, both men and women, by the fear that family is a vacuum that sucks away our own visions, families domesticate us and our dreams. We fear we will become only mothers, only fathers. We fear our family will be the one place we are never really known, as we are known among friends and colleagues. We long to avoid the emptiness of families of the fifties, with their rigid identities and lack of personality, or the aimless ricocheting families of the present. How can we make our families the most rooted place, where we can show who we really are, in all our identities, with our own style and gifts? In truth, no other social place, not work, not friendships, allows us such broad range to exhibit our vision of ourselves. If only we would take the stage.

Our presence, our spirit, in the families we make keep them from being simply corporate entities, where, assigned from birth—son, daughter, mom, dad—everybody gets in their spots. Certainly, creating a family is not just a reproductive act. We know a supply of people does not a family make. Ourself in family is sacred, each member is. Giving ourselves, using our imaginations, and expanding stock family roles saves us from household alienation. A family is not inherited, it must be created. It must be created out of who we are—our intelligence, our imagination, our own changing interior life. We create ourselves as mothers and fathers, and we will be different mothers and fathers to each child, even in the same family.

What do I bring to my children as a lover of art? First, they must know about a portrait of a little girl by Renoir at the Metropolitan Museum of Art in New York. Renoir, in my opinion, painted something out of his league with this portrait. There must have been angels breathing through his brush bristles. Every time I see that little girl I lust for her to be my own, to comfort the tears he luminously captured on her lower eyelashes, to wipe the shell-perfect cheeks of childhood. I have been tempted to rip it off the wall and run for an exit. My children must know why this painting moves me; and they must shut up and listen to me pontificate even when they've had enough and want to go to the snack bar. That's me. To know someone—even your mother—is wonderful and costly. It requires sacrifice, even on the part of children. And I will wrestle them down to the floor and make them listen. I want to be known by my children, not to be caught as only their mother, but to have an identity in my family, to bring my identity to my family, to have that relationship past child rearing into their adulthood, to change with my children. This is one of the joys that's as old as families, which we modern parents have given away in favor of obsessing about our children.

Knowing our children—knowing anyone, in fact—is a two-way street. We get to know someone based on how they respond to who we are. But, conditioned by best-selling pediatricians, child developmentalists, and therapeutic experts, we listen exclusively to our children, and fail to give back ourselves. In this, we forfeit our part of the equation by probing our children about how they feel and what they want, never letting on an inkling as to how we feel, what we know, what we make of the world, further fueling our exhaustion, guilt, and resentment as parents in a lopsided, unsatisfying relationship. Delight in family can only wither away. No wonder children are mystified. They come wanting us and instead are handed hours, days, and years of being told who they are. "You can be anything," we tell them, and we attempt to aid them in this task by helping them figure out with clocklike precision who they are, and what they feel. This is generous, but too small for a family to make it through a life together. It will only send our children out into who they are and thoroughly away from us. In the end, who children are and what they become does depend on what we give them of our ourselves. Children don't want or need any more than what we want and need—to be in a real relationship, seen and heard.

The other thing that my children must know about art and me can be described in a little courting story involving my husband. He is a lover of art, too, though his love is mostly emotional, not based much on technique. Our children surpassed his artistic skills when they stopped doing stick people. But not me. I revel in technique. My children must know that I am a frustrated (I prefer *blossoming*) painter. When my husband found out about this, and saw some of the work I had done in college, he rushed out and bought me a hundred dollars' worth of paints and brushes. He told me he'd take me anywhere to paint—he'd even stand guard in an iffy neighborhood if I wanted to paint its streets and shops. Okay, okay, okay, I said. Maybe next week. Or the week after. Or . . . After a year he said, "To hell with you. Paint when you want. I give up."

I attempted a few works, but gave up. Since having children, I haven't picked up a brush. Just looking at a can of linseed oil strikes me with guilt. I tell myself that I have put painting on hold because I am too busy, but that is only somewhat true. The truth is also that I am afraid. I really want to be a brilliant painter, but it could be I'm just a notch above average. I don't know yet. And this, too, is what I want my children to know about me, whether they like it or not. That may sound too tough. Children can act bored when you tell them about who you are. But the truth of the matter is that you are a fascinating subject to your children, even in your averageness, even in your failings, because you will always be their point of origin.

To create a family that lasts past the feeding-by-spoon stage, the can-I-borrow-the-car stage, means giving your personality, your identity, your presence, to your children so that they have something to come back to, namely you. That's a family that lasts. Giving one's visions, dreams, and loves to your children, letting them witness and experience them, gives children something to work with, something to respond to, even if their choice, when they get older, is to go in the opposite direction. They need a personality that is there to wrestle with, to engage, in order to define themselves. But guess what? You, too, need a personality to survive raising children. It is your presence as a personality, not a role, not a set of duties, that makes a family cohere beyond obligation. You are giving them real knowledge of yourself that will continue to feed them when you are no longer in the picture, even if you are still on their phone list. I don't, in the end, care if my children love painting and drag their dates to museums, but I do care that they know how much it meant to me.

We will have doubts about our depth of relationships with our children. Questions will haunt us. (If a baby-sitter picks them up at school today, will they be irrevocably damaged?) But to a parent, doubt is a way of asking all the right questions. What we so often experience as doubt is really the process of creating ongoing relationships. It is when we stop doubting, thinking, questioning, in relationships that they die.

AIRPORT BOUNDARIES

Personality, identity, presence, all require not only giving, but taking. You have to take a place in your family, too, to practice your presence. It is a strange effort, practicing ourselves, and a funny way to express the idea because it involves new freedoms, and personal, even odd, boundaries—limits to our relationships with children and partner.

I witnessed a classic modern scene—one that would have shocked our grandparents, but doesn't even raise our eyebrows anymore. Suffering an interminable delay in the airport, an engaging, intelligent father with whom I had been exchanging travel pleasantries was attending only cursorily to his three-year-old boy. The boy was pulling on his father's pant leg, tugging, yanking. All the while, the dad was continuing to chat with that tenacity you acquire as a parent in a conversation with a real adult for a change, eyes locked while your body is being dragged away by your child. Finally the little boy began madly kicking his daddy, and on chatted the dad with only a glance downward while nodding gravely at some small thing I said, though he was nearly being toppled. Unable to contain myself, I cautiously offered, "Oh, sweety, you mustn't kick your daddy, you mustn't ever, ever kick your daddy." To tell the truth, I wasn't sure the father even agreed with me, but I left the scene distressed, thinking, "I bet he never lets his staff at the office treat him that way! How could he let his little boy do that to him?"

Only in the role of parent do we let ourselves be treated like this. Why? Do we do this in the name of developmental forgiveness? But we poor parents are still developing, too. The rhetoric of childhood is that children are incomplete, moving through developmental stages to a satisfactory arrival. But who of us has arrived? When are we ever really complete? We are developing together, together we are all growing up, discovering each other and ourselves. Children have to know that you, too, can only take so much whining, that you definitely, under no conditions, will allow yourself to be kicked, and your relationship, like your last will and testament, is still open to conclusion. A family needs to sense when your particular limitations are looming, not because you all want to avoid a confrontation, but because you do have concrete needs, limits, and cares that are yours alone, that identify you to your family and even to yourself. We have to be willing to brave both pain and conflict (but not kicking) to live in a family—a family has to be fought for, both from the inside and out. Families discover, not through pronouncement or biography, but in the course of a day, what you personally are willing and able to show of your self.

WORK AND PRESENCE

Essential to a lasting family is acknowledging that we will be many things to each other for our whole lives, even past death. We can abandon the old fears that family life will smother us and instead go after fully practicing ourselves in the presence of partner and children. In short, making a family is the best way to present ourselves, to stake our claim to a spot on earth. But "practicing ourselves" in front of our family, what does that mean? To give the essence of ourselves to our children is not necessarily dependent on the amount of time you spend with your children. Here, we must recast the debate over moms who work and those who stay at home with children. This is one of those divisions that turn up damned if you do, damned if you don't, because it is a false one from the start. First, mothers have always been "at work," whether farming, spinning, pioneering, running cottage industries, or investment banking. In history, women have always, of necessity, worked for the welfare of their families, some even forced to leave their children behind to find ways to sustain them. Imagine that pain, next time you come home late from the office.

The real issue with at-home moms and working moms is the struggle for identity. Having children is the most identity-challenging and identity-changing thing women do—starting with pregnancy, when even your body gets an identity change. That should be our first big clue. But we are terrified to face it. Who wants to watch your identity evaporate, which is what having children often feels like? Identity isn't about societal roles, either, (the ones we get stuck with can be more burden than help to us). In fact, if we allow societal roles to determine our identity, we are not really in control, we are accepting a series of masks. We have to ask ourselves the hard questions: Who would I be without this job, without this kid, without this income, without this education?—getting at the core of who we are. We must do this work of identity solely on our own, and it is excruciating work. But no one gets out of it, not even mothers. Babies make you ask, "Well, who am I now?" Though it is currently hot in intellectual theory to say we are nothing but social and cultural constructions, this is not a spiritual truth. Identity is something you build relationship by relationship, not role by role. Families, especially at the young-children stage, are not the pause button pressed down on who you are and what you want to pursue. Yes, we may have to put off finishing that degree, taking the promotion that requires weekly travel, writing that screenplay, or finally learning French, but those things weren't going to make you *you* anyway. Your relationships make you who you are, because they give you a chance to actually manifest yourself, and what you really believe in. We fill up what we do with who we are. What we do can never fill us up.

Unfortunately, depending on which choice we've made, to work, or stay home, we get shunted to one camp or the other, like marked creatures. Even women do this to each other. Working moms so often feel they have to justify their choice and struggle profoundly, painfully, with the lack of time with their children. At-home moms feel they might as well just be a large walking dishrag, for all the status and value they are ascribed. We can hardly talk to each other because we feel we lead such different lives, but, sisters, be kind to one another because you may find yourself in the other camp someday.

I still squirm when I think about an encounter I had at a playground not long after I decided to stay home with my third child, having felt I'd earned it after working full time through two other children's preschool years. There I was, a Saturday morning, exhaustedly swinging my up-all-night six-month-old, when the mother swinging next to me started to converse. We chatted about sleep habits, teething, baby bald spots; we joked, we lamented, we laughed. She was funny and smart. But finally the dreaded question came. "So, where do you work?" With the images in mind of having just laboriously hauled around a twenty-pound baby, carried three loads of laundry up two flights of stairs, and wept over the checkbook before food shopping, I stiffened with the answer. "Ah, at home." "Oh, you're a full-time mom?" she slightly sniffed, no doubt a mite envious of the leisurely time she imagined I had to enjoy my baby. I immediately knew the conversation was about to take a turn down that alley. I wanted to say, "But I'm an anthropologist! I'm writing a BOOK, for God's sake! I have a decade of graduate education that I'm still paying bills for, my husband shared primary-care parenting with my other children, I don't have any gray hair yet, my children love me, I'M A MODERN MO-THER!" But I didn't say anything, because I saw the litany going through her mind, "She doesn't know what it's like to get up at five-thirty A.M., pack the breast pump, the briefcase, the kiddy lunch box for day care, write my child's name in the raincoat so it won't be lost again, haul out the car seat, manage the separation scene at day care, face, ON TIME, the uncooperative co-workers who already question my commitment, and hope the phone doesn't ring about that very slight ear infection; to be always competent, inspired, and talented on the next assignment, *before* I think up dinner, once again, from the take-out scene." The national debate divided us on the spot, and I fell for it, diving for cover into my identity as if it were defined by what I do with my time during the day.

It is not the lack of time that crushes our family lives, it is the lack of presence, stricken as we are with tasks, anxieties, and guilt. But between parenting, spousing, cleaning up, working, and carving out a minute or two for yourself—things that each and every one of us struggles with—how, in these conditions, do you give yourself to your children? This is how: by being present—not in every moment; God forbid, we're already exhausted—but in activities such as play, spiritual discussions, tender physical attention, and little daily rituals that can see us through the pace of life today to a strong, coherent, *lived* family life.

IDENTITY HAS YET MANY FACES

Identity is about integration—we can avoid fractured pictures that get seen by the world, or the horrible costume changes we feel we have to make from patient, loving mother, to successful career woman, to smart conversationalist, to savvy businesswoman, to funny, sexy wife. Practicing ourselves, showing ourselves, creating ourselves in front of our children, allows us to be many things to our families, more than just mothers and fathers. Our life with our family is the hub where all the spokes of our identities come together. Our children and our partner can know us in ways impossible from any other angle.

Though I do research and write, few of my colleagues know how I long to teach. My daughter sometimes used to tease me when we were alone: instead of calling me Mom, she'd call me "Madame Professeur," a fancy name learned from a children's picture book. She pronounced this with the goofy accent of a seven-year-old New Yorker. She also said it with a twinkle in her eye because she knows what I aspire to. Still, I may not get to teach. She's the one who has seen a true part of me, of what I believe in, that may never be ratified elsewhere. In this, she sees me as more than her mom, she has seen that I have multiple identities that are beyond her alone.

I remember being strongly affected as a child, saddened almost, and knowing I held a specific bit of information about my father as he recounted for me his young-man longings to go to college to train to be a chemical engineer. But the Depression intervened, and like so many men and women of his generation, he had to winnow down his aspirations. Nobody else ever thought of my father as a chemical engineer, but in my little seven-year-old heart, I held that spot for him. But it was only a spot; the rest of my heart was flooded with the wonderful man he embodied, qualities I can't describe because they were uniquely his, there are no words for them. Now that he's died, I say to people who ask about my father, "He wanted to be a chemical engineer, but he never got to," keeping alive a small spot of him that he never got to claim in life. Here's one of those cases where parallel stories run in families, proving that family life is more strangely patterned than Gothic novels. My father's dream to be a chemical engineer and mine to be a professor are secret identities alive only to our families.

Victor Hugo's theory was: You will know a man not by what he did, but by his dreams. He was onto something, because knowing someone's dreams and their hopes about themselves is an important part of knowing someone. It is one of the telling identities, the multiple facets of seeing someone. To be seen by our spouses, our children, in many ways, as a full, richly textured presence keeps them coming back over a lifetime. We have to keep beguiling, enticing, our families into our many layers of identity. The best way to do this is to tell stories about yourself, your childhood, your day. Amazingly, these stories often teach not only your family who you are, but you too. Such is the power of storytelling.

A PLACE FOR EVERYBODY

Family is a place, but it's never the same place. Families that last make room for each other to pass through and accumulate many identities. To do this they must reimagine, reconvene, their lives together many times. Change, not stability, is the hallmark of a family that lasts. We live not only in the present with one another, but will live together in the future as well, and beyond that, in our memories of each other.

We can conceptualize family life as a kind of architecture, a building now under construction, but with future use in mind. Raising children when they are young is like foundation work for a building—a hell of a lot of backbreaking work, like excavation. What makes this digging easier and more engaging is imagining the building as it rises. It's the same with raising our children. You imagine them at different stages of construction. When you see the experience of child rearing in this breadth of vision, you do it with a new level of dignity, grace, and flexibility, both for yourself and your children. You are not just the ditchdigger; you are also the architect. It's a unique kind of husbandry, planning a place for the future. Building lasting families requires this advance thinking. If we begin our family life with this in mind, we live everyday life with each other in a higher way. I treat my five-year-old differently when I imagine the little boy I address now as a man who will return home. Somehow it seems there is enough time, his whole lifetime, in fact, for him to get his socks on.

We are too locked into the thinking that we raise children

until they are adults, say eighteen, and then they go out and live their own life. Our new life expectancies, however, mean we will live out our lives with our adult children more commonly and longer than any previous generation. It means we have to think out our long-term relations with our children in new ways. Family lifespan has really changed. Though, of course, there have always been children who've had aged parents until late in their lives, that was the unusual case; now it will be the norm. How will we fill up this new time in family life? Continuing to play out the role and duties of a traditional family will not be enough, we have to broaden our relationship with children and raise them from the start with lots of different conceptions of us and each other. Thinking over the long haul means, too, we escape the dread that our mistakes will forever damage the ones we love. Instead, we have multiple chances, multiple identities, multiple moments to forgive. We've been given more time.

When my daughter was a newborn, and I was still an "uncooked" mother, I had one of those inevitable, pathetic, lost days. I yelled, no, screamed, with frustration's edge, at this package-of-noodles baby, who'd materialized faster than instant soup. She blinked back at me. I was shocked at myself and immediately knew I had to apologize. But how do you say sorry to a swaddled lump that does not yet have linguistic comprehension? Are you even supposed to? I certainly knew she'd never tell on me. I stood at the intersection of living one kind of family life or an entirely different one. I decided to give her a place to be the offended party, whether she understood or not. I decided to desert the role of an always competent parent, one who has the last say, always being in the right, even when wrong. It suddenly felt very urgent to me to reset myself. I was thinking of future exchanges when she could speak, when she would know that my behavior was wrong. Carefully and loudly, I said, "I'm sorry I yelled," to a lumpy pink blanket. It is humbling to apologize to an infant, and I am glad it is so. I'd like to think when I'm an old lady in a fuzzy wrap, I'll still have the necessary wisdom to apologize to my daughter.

COLLECTIVE IDENTITY AND STEW

A collective identity is made up, like good stew, of the distinctive qualities each family member brings—not just their outward characteristics, but also the accumulated experiences, even traumas, that a family passes through in its span of time together. As we each have many roles to play in our families, our collective identity, too, undergoes many transformations. We had tumultuous departures in our house during our first few years of family life. Somebody was always mad by the time we got out the door. Whoever misplaced keys, whoever was still busy grooming, all suffered various shades of blame and irritation. We were The Late Family. One day we found a sign posted by some anonymous family member (could it have been Daddy? Mommy perhaps?) on the back of the front door. It said "EXIT WITH DIGNITY." This presented the possibility of a new identity for us. Somehow, we all obeyed.

Creating a family that lasts, creating an identity together that lasts, is certainly an ongoing project. We *will* go through stages together, and we will watch each other doing it—stages of marriage, stages of childhood, unfold, develop, close. We will change shape through addition and loss, but an identity together can never be lost, it can always be remembered and recalled. We passed through the Late Family stage. We laugh about it now, its frustration can't hurt us anymore. It has, instead, become a memory to reflect on, to tease each other with, to remind us that we did something together—even if it was being late.

Some families have identities wrapped around passions. Down the street from us is the Chess Family. I swear they must eat, dream, and breathe chess. Their little boy is a touring contender, their father has become a masterful coach. The four-year-old girl can sweetly tell you why you are about to make the wrong move. This collective identity has given them a core, a new kind of hearth around which to gather. Not every moment, of course—they do other things; but as something they do together passionately, it draws them together down the long road of a lifetime family with lasting interests. I know the Quintet Family, too, all string players, and I stand in special awe of them. Nothing, it seems to me, is quite as moving as watching them play their instruments together, though I know in my heart they have paid for it with countless hours of squeaky, relentless practice. My favorite story about them is the time the mother came across a music store going out of business. She bought out their stock of violins, all sizes, because it was cheaper to own one in every size than rent each size as all her children grew into the next stage. She had to rent a van to get them all home. They love to explain that they had to move to a larger house to hold all the violins, but secretly, I think that's a bit of a story they tell to ensure their family identity as passionate musicians together.

The care and tending of a collective identity is especially powerful for families trying to pull together after divorce, remarriage, or death. Families in these circumstances, it may be recalled, have been a traditional type of family in history because death was so prevalent and took away so many spouses, in childbirth, in labor accidents—all so very common that remarriage was the order of the day, and almost always with attendant children. These families had something going for them that families today often do not. They *had* to stick together to survive. Husbands who lost wives and had children needed to have another mother for them and remarried quickly; wives losing husbands had, quite often, no form of support except through a second marriage. They knew they had to make it as a family or face poverty. The novels of George Eliot, Jane Austen, Dickens, Thackeray, Trollope, are filled with families where stepchildren, stepparents, half-brothers and -sisters, were common and family settings were complicated. It's nice to know that the stuff that makes for great literature is the same stuff that makes a family. Ellen Ross, social historian and author of *Love and Toil: Motherhood in Outcast London, 1870–1918*, charts the course of adoption, remarriage, separation, and a myriad of household arrangements in Victorian England, confirming how common these families were and that they are not wholly unlike today's equally complicated families. What holds families together under complex circumstances is often pressure from without. But we don't need tragedy; we can build coherent families from within by forming collective identities arising from the interests and passions of family members.

FAMILY CULTURE AND SPIRIT

We will always be in families, all cultures give us that. Kinship by blood or kinship by marriage will outlast all the predictions of their demise. We are, nevertheless, living through another age of tremendous change in form, with all the opportunities to shape our own families more personally. Mobility and fewer children have unhooked us from the netting of extended families that once made claims upon us. While we experience more freedoms from the models of the past, along with the losses, we are still trying to figure out where to go to make our own family cultures.

However, we do know already what we don't want to lose, we do know what sustains. Culturally and personally, we have arrived at a time where we need not only new flexibilities, but also lasting things. A family's own culture will be shaped through shared meaning, old and new; its memories; its imagination, and a family spirituality. All are necessary to make a personal family culture.

Family spirituality is an especially hard concept to claim. In our age of diversity and individuality, and unlike previous ages of majority traditions, it is hard to find a common definition. We only know we've got to have it. For some it's formal worship, for others it is an evening meal indulged in, oblivious of time. For others it is a conversation that, for its brief life, is immune to old hurts. Spirituality is profoundly connected to discovering meaning, and if we can understand how to activate meaning, we begin to get at our own life of spirituality as well. Uncovering, creating, and assigning meaning to the everyday nourishes this kind of timeless spirituality.

I learned my lesson through a friend. She had a miscarriage—a pregnancy very much wanted and enthused over. When rushed to the white emergency room, this couple was shattered out of their heretofore happy-go-lucky life—all before had gone so well. In this clinical place, while being discharged, the woman, desperately, without thinking, insisted on keeping the little "sample" collected in the aftermath. She hadn't yet comprehended that she was supposed to let go. A kind nurse told her to hide it under her gown, for it wasn't hospital policy to release such materials. She left with a tiny embryo in a small medical vial. When she made it home, she was horrified. What was she to do with this object? I was mortified myself to hear her story. Yet, in this instance, ritual came to her aid, and after some discussion, she told me that she and her husband took this astonishingly small creature, placed it in a still silk-lined milkweed pod from a dried flower arrangement, tied it shut with thread, and early the next morning buried it quietly, surreptitiously, in a neighborhood garden. With it they also buried one rose thorn—to express both the beauty and pain of life.

She has since had other miscarriages, but expressed that she did not again feel the need to act for each in the same way; her memory served to heal the rest. What I learned from her, profoundly, was to acknowledge what happens to us, to our families, and insist on significance out of chosen moments. We will remember them naturally, instinctively. But *chosen* acknowledgment—this heals and binds us, allowing us to pour ourselves back into life again. Acknowledgment is a special kind of knowledge—it belongs to a family of words that include *acceptance, admitting, assenting;* it is "to grant," "to recognize." To acknowledge what happens to us, between us, as families, is to win a life's wisdom, an existential, personal wisdom, claimed no other way.

We are constantly longing for meaning, looking here and lamenting there while secretly knowing that it is we ourselves who have to make it, to reclaim it from lost places. We can reframe the lament *What does this really mean?* by providing our own. By starting a family of our own we finally get to make the meaning of our relationships, of our traditions. These meanings are the natural expression of our imagination and emotions, indeed, only we can give them. And nowhere does imagination need more presence than in building a life together as a family. Imagination—not only the fun, crayon kind, but as a deeply felt, broad vision—gives us to each other in new ways, opening up new landscapes for us to occupy.

IMAGINATION AND FAMILY CULTURE

Imagination needs forums to appear in. It is in our daily care of each other, in our spirituality, in our play together, in our rituals, in our physical homes, that we can give our imaginations full reign. How we implement this, how we allow it to take root in our lives, will be distinctive to each family, but encouraging imagination in the everyday is essential.

Imagination is a product of inspiration, it is always on the lookout to make something happen, something usually delightful and delicately wrought. If we train our imagination on our families, we make our life not only endurable, but enjoyable, along with all the tasks and conflicts that we probably wish we could imagine out of existence. Imagination is so often associated with fun because it is the power to create, the power of the generative, to once again give life, as we did in birth. Imagination is a powerful source we have at our free disposal to make family life vivid, engaged, *worth it.*

We are now in our parents' shoes, finding how tough it is to make a family. It's our turn to become the guardians of our own traditions. We are the linking generation for making and maintaining lasting ties. And imagination is at our disposal every day through language.

CHATTER AND LANGUAGE

In all cultures, it turns out, chatter is one of the heights of human achievement. Talk is fundamentally human and fundamentally spiritual. Little talk, big talk—talk is what families do. So many of our longings about families have to do with talking. And talk requires effort and practice. All those little conversations add up. Talk is what you will do at their cribside and they at your bedside. To speak of anything, anything at all, is an important marker of intimacy, and that is what we all want from families. To think back to our own family lives is to wish simply that there had been more talk. It comes as no big surprise how much children want to talk. They stampede you with words for the first five years, yet how do we keep the conversation alive for a lifetime? Believe it or not, your family has its own dialect.

A dialect is one of the most precious treasures in a family's trove. The place to start any language is nouns. Our pet names for each other, whether they change over time or remain constant, will go with us to death. My mother-in-law's father, in an Alzheimer's haze, never once failed to call her by her childhood name, La Piccina—my little one—though he often did not know his own. Names of this kind are infinitely malleable, and they can, in an instant, charge the atmosphere with humor or gravity.

A family's language must comprise more than names or words, of course. It will be an atmosphere, a style, a distinct way of doing, part of your identity. Every family has its language, but acknowledging it, nurturing it, and building it puts it at our service.

What face we show to the world as a family will probably be conventional, comprising polite manners, clean clothes, and some semblance of stolid respectability, but our private voices to each other can be just as goofy as we want. The language we use with each other can take flight into outer space, if need be, to satisfy our communal compulsion to speak to each other. I can't even describe for you my family's dialect, it would be totally unintelligible, though you might recognize some of the accents as Bronx Italian, Hungarian Rhapsody, Tina Louise Tinsel, Mobster Mash.

With all this cacophony, I can say that, thankfully, family dialects are also built with silence. A wave of new brain research reports the importance of speaking to your children from infancy to age three to produce smart, creative, adaptable kids. True, but we want our kids to be more than smart, we want them to be wise, and for wisdom one needs many languages, not only the spoken one, but the silent as well. Your father may have been the most silent of men, but you know he communicated something, too, often in his silence.

American Indians raise their children with far less speaking, but their silence is voluminous.

A stretched-out afternoon with everyone preoccupied in his own project, buzzing in and out of the same rooms, has a special effect of intimacy. As a person can relax completely when alone, so, too, families must, corporately, be able to be alone together. Allowing silence is a vital part of family language.

We need many languages, family tailored, and those languages can be the languages of play, ritual, touch, prayer, food, silence. Just as we expect depth in the articulation of our spoken word as we grow, it is possible to communicate more potently, with more articulation, over time, in each of these other languages.

MEMORY AND THE FUTURE

Memory carries meaning into the future. Like fallen leaves, memory accumulates naturally, but by raking and composting we can take advantage of its elemental power today. We can assist memories to do their work. We can store up memories for each other by everyday things, using them as cues. We have a little neighbor, about nine, who called frantically, seeking the too-small bike he'd given us last year. He had decided that he wanted it back. "I want to save it for my little boy when he grows up," he apologized in his squeaky voice. Alas, the bike had long since passed on from us to other hands, but this boy already had something to offer his progeny of far greater worth. He was intuitively practiced at memory, using it to make a relationship with the imagined son of his future.

We don't have to let this natural ability fade away from us as adults. We can also work consciously, marking parties, special evenings, songs, books, really anything at all, to create meaningful memories. It is traditional to cherish and hand on family heirlooms like jewelry and tea sets. These objects do a lot more work than serving tea. When you pour that cup, Great-Aunt Gretchen suddenly hovers over the table, claiming you, weaving you into her tapestry of family.

But memory cues don't have to be limited to objects, they can attach to experiences, too. Lucy was born to music; her parents, musicians, had recorded the slow second movement of Dvořák's *New World Symphony* to calm her mom during labor. But this is Lucy's piece of music, and as she has grown older, she judiciously allows it to be played at certain occasions special to her. Her parents already know they will have to find a small ensemble for her graduation party, only hoping, among their circle of friends, there will be those capable of handling the *New World Symphony.* The memory of this music will be loomed through Lucy's life, accumulating richly as it goes. So many potential moments like Lucy's are passed over in our rush of life, and all family members don't pay the same kind of attention to revealing moments. But if we are in the practice of accumulating many of them, being alert to their periodic appearance, though we miss some, enough will also get through.

FAMILY AND TIME

We build up family over time, yet there is a window of opportunity that also restricts us. We are limited in our various stages, whether as new couples or as new parents, but what we have left is memory. While we have all the time we need, every moment, too, is urgent. We must claim our moments—given, found, or made by us. Otherwise our blind routines will consume the time given.

Family life is a stream, and we can jump in anywhere along its course. It doesn't have to start at the wedding or the moment the first child is born. It is never too late to practice imagination, to bring oneself in a fresh way to family life. Words are not even necessary.

For example, a widowed professor we know, an elegant, polished man, visits his aging immigrant mother once a week. They have always had a stormy relationship. She doesn't understand his modern life and so he has little to say to her. For these visits, he brings bakery cake. He'd rather they talked, but they can't; instead they prepare a setting—place mats, forks, paper napkins, plates—letting the preparation take up a great deal of time, and they sit and eat this cake together. That's what they do, and through it, their little family is carried forward. He did not begin bringing cakes until after he was sixty.

Perhaps you think of this story as a sad one—it is, in its own way—for you wish for this elderly mother and her adult, dignified son to have more together at this stage of their lives; but if you see it as sad, it's because you already know what the problem is—that we want more from our families, we want them to be a true home to us, true rest, a place for our true selves. And if you don't see this tale as sad, it's because you take the hope that's there. We can, even late in life, even with our history of mistakes, still begin little ways to be together. I include it to show that we need to be ready, all our lives, to get to that place. We can start with cake. It may end with only cake. But it's cake, and everyday things like it, that carry us as families. It carried the good professor and his mother, and it can carry us too.

Two

The Meaning of Play

*I*t's strange to begin a chapter on the meaning of play with a story of death, but it shows us, somehow, that play is sacred.

Surrounding their aged father's hospital bed, machines all finally silenced, a long wait coming to a close, two daughters and a son who have said all their good-byes, exchanged all remorses, finalized reconciliations, begin to sing. There isn't anything else, really, to do. He can't talk anymore, and neither can they. They start the song a little awkwardly, choosing something comforting and familiar, an old ditty learned from him as children, sung from summers past spent romping at Cape Cod. As their voices join and rise up, they sing with all their memories flooding forward, coming to their aid. When they get to the last verse, out of nowhere, the father struggles, half upright, to finish the song with them. The next day, he dies. The song remains, of course, but, for the son, the daughters, it is utterly transformed from a simple childhood chant, a pastime, to the gift given for their father's final journey.

Play, as we think of it today, is far too utilitarian, lost to its ancient universal, anthropological powers. Modern economy has squeezed out the inspired, exalted, spirit-awakening aspects of play, underestimating it. Play is transcendent, a sure mark of the sacred, but we leave it mostly to children, preferring to go on to more important things. Yet singing, dancing, clapping, chasing each other, dress-up and disguises, which we mostly think of as children's games, can all come back to possess us, even at the very end of our adult lives, in very adult ways. Play doesn't become sacred with age; it is that way from the beginning. In short, we live with a cheap view of play, severed from its far more central, spiritual elements. Indeed, there are some scholarly, serious, and grown-up people who happen to think of play as a most, perhaps *the* most, important thing humans do.

"To dare, to take risks, to bear uncertainty, to endure tension—these are the essence of the play-spirit," wrote Johannes Huizinga, Dutch historian, in his seminal work, which identified mankind, foremost, as creatures of play. In this work, titled *Homo Ludens: (homo ludens* is Latin for "mankind as the species of play") *A Study of the Play Element in Culture,* Huizinga sees the role of play in human life not as something incidental or even developmental, but rather as fundamental—always and to all ages.

Huizinga's theories are truly radical. He suggests, for example, that culture arises, not out of suffering, as novels and movies tell us, but out of play. Play is quite serious business to Huizinga, the rector of Leyden University in his day. His ideas become all the more fascinating when one considers that he lived and lectured from *Homo Ludens* during the Nazi occupation of Holland. He viewed play as a way to fight for elemental humanness.

Webster gives the following synonyms for play: "frolic," "jest," "flutter." These are hardly verbs that one associates with a way to fight evil. But play is subversive in that it undermines the sinister, which is always serious. It punctures a hole in inauthentic power. Take for example the sheer glee in watching Jack Nicholson play a mental inmate in *One Flew Over the Cuckoo's Nest;* or the characters of *M*A*S*H,* who use play to combat the devastation of wartime grief and absurdities.

Yet today we mildly think of play for adults as a way to unwind. It's the balanced counterpoint to work. We keep it in a separate category, "after work." We no longer wind it in and out of our day, singing as we go. But play is not really the opposite of work—indeed, the best work springs up from play. Work is not higher than play, it's really the other way around. Play turns work on its head, it takes out the grind. Play is the best thing we can do, especially in our work, and most especially in the work of raising families. Play is imagination made manifest; humor equipped to strike; creativity injected back into the domestic day. It rivals the gods in power. The wisest people know this and live this. Ancient sages spinning myths always furnished them with humor. The Southwest Indians' favorite wise character is the Trickster, who propels himself through life by farting. Perhaps you don't think of that as funny; if you don't, take two doses of the closest comic book with a glass of bubbling beer and retire to your couch. No comic books in your house? Try Chaucer's

"The Miller's Tale." Chaucer agreed with Huizinga that play is a shot at high art.

As adults, we need to reconsider play. We cannot leave play behind for children. Undoubtedly the father dying in the sterile hospital bed never expected to be attended by true children singing, and singing a ditty, no less. Though they were his "adult" children at his side, nonetheless, they were children, and he, too, in that moment, was again a child.

Play returns us all to childhood and therein lies its sacredness, its blessedness. It shows us at our most elemental, as a body radiating mind and imagination. Children and play are inseparable for a reason: to be at play is an experience of unconscious authenticity, of our effervescent and unique wholeness. These are facts children never stray far from. Playing restores us to smallness in a big, big world, full of possibilities as we humbly look on. It's an experience of our completeness, calling us out into life's adventures, making us ready to fight not only the bad guys, but their pals—tedium, weariness, and crankiness (both children's and parents').

Maybe doing laundry is not fighting evil (in your experience), but I know that having the children "help" me by lining up and throwing freshly washed clothes into buckets labeled with each one's name gives a little levity to a long day. Carting the buckets off to the drawers is also fun for the toddler set, though I have to explain over and over to my husband why he so often has to search for clean underwear somewhere in the bottom of a bucket. Play can, and should, if we understand it, be woven into our daily life, in among our daily acts.

Play is voluntary—unlike the demands of work. Work is something you do for a wage, something you earn, but play you do from your spirit. You earn a wage, you give to your play—one plays music, plays ball, these are like acts of love, spontaneously generous. It is not by chance that *play* is the noun used for great dramas or the common verb used with music or great athletic games. *Put on a play, play the cello,* or *Play ball!*—usually uttered with great seriousness—are phrases expressing anticipation of how we will be carried up and away, the burdens of life lifted from us.

Play, too, is irreplicable; you may play the same game, but the outcome is different every time. In our mechanical age of reproduction, we've left behind the electrifying bang of the irreplicable moment, the inspired spark of imaginative connection, of things coming together once in a lifetime, which are all the materials out of which play, indeed all great creations, are made. Creating new and unexpected relationships between things, ideas, experiences, places, people, is inherently playful. The serendipity of two unexpected colors colliding on a canvas, characters of a story turning an abrupt corner, of musical instruments bumping their sound out at one another, are all sources of play. Jaw-dropping athletic feats can never be performed again, no matter the instant replay. Out of the magical properties of these moments come flights of delight and spinning wholeness that, once past, astonish us with their innocence. We never quite expected, when we picked up that stuffed animal, the tale that tumbled out of us, animating its furry little life. And though it may not have been a Pulitzer Prize story, the attempt alone erased the day's cynicism. We've been visited by play. We're back in the world of possibilities. In our human urge we try to capture this feeling over again, secure its consistency, cage the bird. We record performances, rewind and replay, and demand that all our experiences of this kind be consistently available for us whenever we want them. We want the same effect every time. We want standardized magic. But this is not play because play is an adventure, with the outcome unknown. All we can do is go on until the next time. Play is an attitude, not a goal, not a product. You cannot buy play, you can only buy the setting and hope it happens. We've all been there, the time you set up the circumstances, the setting, to have a great time and it didn't happen. Play is definitely like a visitation, like an angel; you don't know when it will come, it might not come when you invite it, but if it appears, be ready to host it, and to improvise.

In those passed-around stories about birthday fiascos, one father tells his story of every parent's panic: the planned games were over far too quickly, seventy-five long minutes before pickup. Ten bored children were staring at him. He rattled around in a panic, reflexively opening the fridge to gaze in at the possibilities, a classic act of stress relief. Spying a can of whipped cream, he seized it, pulled up a high stool, and invited the guests to be "shaved." Spraying whipping cream all over children's faces, one at a time, and elaborately scraping them with a butter knife (make sure to hold their noses, for effect, and slip into open squealing mouths at least one blob of cream) and wiping excess on a hand towel has got to go down as a masterly inventive moment. Improvisation, in fact, is a necessary condition to play; humor cannot move forward without improvisation, it only turns stale and hardens. Being willing to act with the materials at hand is as necessary to play as it is to wilderness survival. As distant as they seem from one another, play and survival are closer cousins than we think. Resourceful humor is probably as urgent a skill to pass on to children as that week at Camp Flintfire; and habitual play will do it.

As parents, we are conditioned to think of play as motor-building skills, or as comprising activities that help children practice for adulthood. We view play as an activity that will get kids out of our hair—most adults purchase toys so kids can entertain themselves. We struggle to enjoy sitting down and playing with our kids, especially once they move from the cute-because-it's-the-first-time to an age where they can sustain play themselves—we see that as time when we can finally get some work done—and are torn when kids continue to want us to play with them. Play for children is not just about practicing to be grown up; just as play for adults is not solely about getting to be kids again—though, thank goodness, that's there too. Play for children, and for adults, is about conquering the world in front of them, proceeding into the landscape laid out for an adventure. You begin to see how we could, as adults, want play as part of our daily life as much as children do.

ADULT PLAY

If we do get around to thinking about play for adults, our expectations are conditioned to follow the same path as current child's play. We've let play for adults become just as utilitarian. It has to serve a purpose. Adult play is done either for stress relief, health reasons, or, ringing even more hollowly, it's narrowly aimed at a sexualized result—that getaway weekend promising the candlelight dinners and a hotel room with a heart-shaped tub. This limited view of play compromises not only our family lives, but adversely affects our marriages. Not that there's anything wrong with a husband and wife whose play is a tough round of tennis. But ideally, there is a larger understanding that will sustain them both as individuals and lifelong partners.

What, then, is the essential core of play? How exactly does play "work"? What does a rich appreciation of play accomplish in relationships and in families? The best place to answer this is not by looking at the obvious source of child's play, but first at the possibilities of adult play. Plus, in our world, it's where play is needed most.

It is helpful, even encouraging, in this discussion of adult play to recall that it has long existed in previous cultures. We know the Greeks played not only great games but great dramas and comedies. Imagine, too, Crow Indians playing ball and stick games, something akin to softball. For both cultures, play was not solely about leisure time, or socialization—that is, using games in a utilitarian way to teach youngsters their future place in society. Play was about sociability—the joy of being together. Gathering to play was and should be lighthearted, restorative, and delightful. Adult play is not a modern pursuit invented for the affluent elderly in Florida. James Atlas, in notable essay in *The New Yorker*, asks, "Where has all the fun gone?" He equates adult fun with sex, drugs, and rock and roll, and especially, staying out late. Of the four, he got only one right, but he's too tired, having children, to stay out late. Yes, we're too tired these days to stay out late; we have to switch around our old party-animal notions of adolescent fun and stay out late in the middle of the afternoon. As Mark Twain knew, real fun is playing hooky and pretending you're somebody else.

A woman whose husband is an amateur architecture buff gets him each year, by hook or crook, a tour of a building he has admired, for his birthday present. The plans begin months before the big day, when he sends her an "anonymous" postcard with only an address scrawled on it. Her mission: get him to the top, the very top, of that building. Certainly, this event could be considered a ritual, and a beautiful one, because it's an annual event, but along with that, it's sheer play.

The couple, who live in New York City, don't choose well-known structures like the Empire State Building or World Trade Center but, rather, lesser-known edifices whose owners give tours to no one but building inspectors. It is her job to find a way to get in, and to do this she usually poses as an architecture student (she is a secretary) doing research on the chosen building.

First, she goes to the library and looks up any existing information on the building: year built, architect, special features, and so on. Then she calls the owner, who's usually suspicious, but talks her way in by providing the owner with a wealth of detail that almost always has been lost over the years and through the passage to new owners. The owner agrees—perhaps he even thinks her information on the building's history will allow for higher rents.

She and her husband show up on the appointed day. And now the action begins. She is the student and he poses as her photographer. Year after year they go to the nooks and crannies of these buildings; they go places where no pigeon has ever gone before: towers, balconies, pinnacles. Whenever the owner balks at showing them some feature, she says, pointing to her husband, "I think George, here, would need to get a few shots from the roof to catch the effect of the sun on your valuable terra cotta." And off they go.

When the two finish, the baby-sitter's schedule permitting, they go off to celebrate, she with a martini, he with a beer and a cigar. This annual event feeds them the entire year because by occupying this once-a-year identity, for a few hours living beyond their typical character, they actually draw closer together. They have played together. He has seen her have to think fast on her feet when the owner asks her when she expects to finish her degree, and she has had to watch her husband, a totally nonmechanical man, effect a light-meter reading. They marvel at each other. And this is one of the treasures of play.

The good thing about this, in the face of the sexualization of twentieth-century culture, is that this is not *foreplay*. If there is a sector of society that has attempted to capitalize on the idea of play, it is the sex industry. Every mall in America has a boutique with intimate wear designed to bring out the playfulness in your mate. Big-city streets boast shops that feature a wide variety of sex "toys." What is good about sex toys is that, in many cases, they invite the user to put on a new identity for a while. What's bad about them is that so many are really devices geared toward steering an encounter to a preordained event—sex. Play, on the other hand, is an unlimited adventure, with more than the body at stake. Play—as sex can, but often doesn't—asks us to use all of our capacities.

Ironically, sexuality often shoves play out of marriage. Sex has become the "objective" in romance, in the same way that "motor-skill building" has become the objective in child's play. These objectives are not in themselves negative, of course, but they are bad when they squeeze all other aspects of fun out of the relationship. Play is a way to fight back. Play provides new ways of being together, and not so as to escape ourselves, but to bring more of ourselves to each other—as did the couple on the building tour.

Our ability to play with our partner is a sure mark of the strength and breadth of our relationships, especially as we are further compressed between unrelenting, culturalized sexualization on one side and overwhelming family responsibilities on the other. Lovers who play together develop new ties to each other, surpassing sexuality alone, by showing each other new faces. This is not to say that play will not renew their physical attraction. Yes, play is an aphrodisiac, only because all good aphrodisiacs are really about more than momentary stimulation, they produce sustained attraction. Nonetheless, if you do want to enliven your sex life through play, forget the sex shops and visit a real toy store. Play is by nature more expansive, it goes well beyond the physical. It gives us new sites of love, unpredictable places and moments of the unexpected where we can be together beyond the daily grind of who we "usually" are. Playing together as lovers is a continued courtship, a coaxing and inviting beyond the ways in which you already know each other. We can literally create new identities with each other, and therefore new kinds of intimacy. One couple we know took a fresh look at each other when the wife, dressed as a trench-coated detective with a fedora pulled low over her brow, arrested her husband as he exited his office building, shuffling him off for a "private interrogation" at a close-by coffee shop. The excuse "Oh, I could never do something like that" fades when one understands the value of playfulness. In ways like this, play grants new possibilities and illumines secluded worlds, yet unimagined, for us to play in. The most vulnerable moment of play is when someone says, "Will you play with me?" It is the moment of an exposed longing, and if the invitation is accepted, new intimacies are formed and new playscapes are created. While we adults don't ask our partners in such a literal way, we can duplicate the same experience of childhood. We do need each other to play.

We've carefully watched, for a number of years now, an elderly couple take their daily walk in our neighborhood park. They first attracted our attention because they often held hands, oblivious to us, plunged, as they were, in deep and jovial conversation. What, we wondered, could they still be saying to each other after all these years? He would look at her so expectantly, smiling broadly and with triumph. Our curiosity was further piqued when we discovered he is a world-famous law professor, stooped, yes, but still teaching; she, a former kindergarten teacher. Slowly, as we got to know them, only as passing strollers, mind you, our curiosity became unbearable, and one day we called out, "Why are you two always laughing?" He turned, eyes glistening, and replied, "Oh, I tell her a recent case, and she turns it into a movie musical!" Their daily walk, it turns out, was their playtime, she turning his work world into comedies to amuse him and, no doubt, herself. Lest the thought of this exhausts you, I am sure they didn't start out, as youthful lovers, able to construct entire cross-genre productions during a constitutional walk in the park. Maybe they only started by imagining a smug judge with the ears of the literal ass that he was, but I am sure that over the years they surprised themselves with their capacity to build up more elaborate, comedic pleasures for each other. The result: fifty years of playing together, still holding hands.

Now, that is seduction. Don't tell me play isn't more sexy than sex.

Maybe your moment of breakthrough will be buying a rubber fish and planting it in a bowl of water to fake out your family, but let me persuade you that what you've just done is related to the sacred. You may buy a melting gel capsule that explodes into a miniature foam-sponge chicken and drop it in your partner's Saturday morning cappuccino, but if you've made a human laugh, gods are smiling. You are now operating at the pinnacle of sophistication, because humor is the most elusive, intelligent, delicate, frothy, ardent concoction of a human mind. Watch a Charlie Chaplin movie if you want to get a sense of the divine genius of play. Watch it with your children and you'll find yourself surprised that you laugh together at exactly the same moments. We know we've reached the absolute core of humanity when something makes both children and adults squeak, squeal, and guffaw. Humor, comedy, and play are crowning paradoxes of human experience, because life is filled with so much labor and pain. To laugh is victory, to play, Godlike. Frothlike though they may be, humor, comedy, and play are at the toughened core of survival, allowing us to advance into age with grace.

My elderly, strolling lovers were playing together through the time-honored tradition of storytelling, as in *Tales of the Arabian Nights*. Completing each other's stories, layering on new episodes, adding invented characters, or talking in play voices or with accents to each other illustrates play's engagement of the imagination.

These devices often lead to previously unknown or unguessed qualities or knowledge about one's partner. A genteel and deeply shy young man used to jolt his wife with his uncharacteristic witty and very biting social comments only while playing a certain card game. Somehow, whenever those cards were fanned out in front of him, some unseen aspect emerged and he postured and reveled in her delighted and raucous prodding.

Play is always very personal; a concoction of your imagination. What kinds of play you invite your partner, or child, or family, to share will be an expression of your interests and loves. You play on your strengths, so to speak, but surprisingly you discover your vulnerabilities, and that is exactly how you grow intimate from playing together. You discover the insecurities and gain trust being silly and gleeful together. But how does one start?—for it takes courage to play. Start small, as children do. Visit a novelty shop.

It is a risk to play. When a young father wanted to teach his four-year-old daughter how to tap-dance, he discovered he had, again, to live through some tough memories of his demanding father teaching him. He found himself surprised that he felt he wasn't good enough to teach his daughter and that she would be critical of his dancing. Yet she was delighted when just presented with the shoes alone. Willing partners, as children usually are, are easy to play with, like it's easy to love those who love you. It's the unwilling partner that's tough—that suited, cranky husband, for example. He may show more irritation than glee at your attempts at play. Go ahead and put salt in the sugar bowl. "Grow up!" he might crack, but like a doctor sure of her diagnosis, persist. This patient needs lifesaving and spontaneous treatment, for a momentary and imaginative crack in routine is the only way to get at play. In fact, turning routine objects to devious ends will usually get you at least a minute of playtime.

What characterizes all play is its ability to lift us out of everyday time and launch us into places of imagination and pleasure without paying the dues of an "objective." When we play together, we rejuvenate our relationships. We add fresh water to the well that is so often sucked dry by the everyday cares of the world. We have become teammates on the playing field instead of opponents. Play suspends the weight of time, if only for an hour or two, while we nurture our imaginations. Children understand this. No six-year-old making a city out of Legos or paper boxes looks over his shoulder at the clock or rides his bike to get his heart rate up to 170 beats per minute. Certainly, we adults must keep track of time and tend to our health. However, we must pause to recognize that play is not solely the domain of children—that we exist in the world of imagination, too.

When do we start to give up play, and why? Somewhere, when enough of life's blows accumulate, the scales tip and we don't think much about playing anymore. For us "grown-ups" to exist in the world of imagination requires special energy and effort, but it comes more naturally the more we try it because it is like coming home.

The time to play is now. In our society, play is acceptable for retired adults. They are allowed to play because they've paid their dues. But that's a small view. Play is something that must be part of our lives regularly. People who work and have children need play as much as ever. It makes work and the daily grind not only more palatable, but more productive. Our longings for the different, the better, and less dulling are satisfied in play, at least for the animated interval. It doesn't have to last long, it can be just a passing fancy. Above all, playing together is not another task to add to the family list.

One time a houseguest of ours produced a commotion when he ran, wrapped only in a towel, out into our kitchen, and grabbed the box of Froot Loops sitting on the breakfast table. He charged back to the bath, where his wife was in the shower, and sprinkled half the box of cereal over the curtain. We heard her squealing, and she came out later looking happy and sheepish. He did this for absolutely no reason that I ever found out (or cared to!). By the way, I no longer buy bagels and cream cheese when they stay with us.

Childhood has another lesson that adults often forget about play: it can be solitary. How many times do we cut ourselves off from an activity because, if seen, it would make us feel foolish? The man who, while cooking alone, dances around his kitchen like a rock-and-roll star, using his spatula as a microphone, has achieved nothing that will make him richer or smarter. But, for a song or two, he's let down his guard, let his imagination soar, and blown off some steam.

Among our other houseguests we count a lovely young woman who preferred to rise up before us early in the morning. It was her pleasure to serve us breakfast with a fake British accent, complete with steeped tea. She would chatter in an Eliza Doolittle voice, performing both the brash cockney flower girl and the elegant, transformed socialite, merrily chirping back and forth between personae, all the while clattering cups and swishing around us with a funny little walk. Then off she'd go to her round of appointments in the art world of New York's SoHo. She can always stay with us.

Because we live in New York City and are in fatal possession of an extra room, we do have a stream of houseguests. Everybody eventually comes through; don't be surprised someday if you find yourself among them. But of all my visitors, one of my most favorite was a pal I went to school with, one of those inventive geniuses whose thoughts are too big for fitting comfortably in any one place. He collected old things, odd things, things no one had known a use for in fifty years. He would come with his rucksack stuffed with unidentifiables that he would parcel out along with explanations, until you were, with him, in wonder of a 1920s metal-jawed jar-grip that could cleverly open any size cap, or a cigar punch shaped as Satan's spear, or a wick-trimmer hidden in a miniature silver box. It was endless, this stream of things he produced. Polished and adored old box cameras, roofing tools, compasses, letterpresses, tin embossers, copper triggers, bootjacks, pen bladders, heavy black telephones surely used to call a film-noir detective. Because he possesses this childlike curiosity coupled with educated brilliance, he can't help but be delighted with the world as he finds it, and find it he does. Objects seem to seek him out, knowing they will be properly appreciated. I take his advanced intelligence as a sign in the right direction, because while he is the only person I know who can find the properties and techniques of smelting antique bronze hidden in episodes of Greek mythology, his instinct is to keep simple play at hand. He might fold a dollar bill into a origami frog while on hold on the phone, making it jump for my kids' amusement. If you dismiss him as an eccentric, you'll have to discard the perfectly plain matron with at least sixty years under her aprong strings. "I keep a pink rubber pig hung up by the sink," she said without hesitation when asked about playfulness. "I just get a charge out of it."

As you can tell from the stories so far, play is not leisure, though you may leisurely plan an attack of play. While leisure is repose, play is active engagement that releases us into new mental spaces, new atmospheres. Play is not entertainment; entertainment is passive, play is active—that is why, when TV replaces children's play, even adult play, something is lost. That something is more than the active practice of imagination, it's also a loss of intimacy, a challenge disappointingly unmet, energy evaporated, a new possibility left untouched, routine further ingrained.

CHILDREN'S PLAY

Adults are the shepherds of children's play. We need to be because, while we understand a three-year-old's fascination with pliers, we know their power to pinch thumbs and noses. Yet, what kind of stewards are we being in our children's play? Surely we can't only be naysayers. More important, we must allow them to play without agendas and expected results.

A mom at her first nursery-school parents' committee got a rude awakening in this regard. The committee's members were discussing what new toys to buy with the school's limited budget. There ensued a very technical debate between those who wanted to purchase ABC blocks, which would build tactile skills, those who wanted to buy the XYZ manipulatives, which would enhance hand-eye coordination, and those who insisted on acquiring a trunkful of medieval costumes, not for fun, but for the guarantee that it would improve the children's self-esteem. The poor woman, who had grown up playing quite happily with the scraps of traditional toys handed down by her older brothers, was shocked. "What about play," she asked herself, "without an objective?" Again, play for play's sake.

On a purely mundane level, certainly, play has educational purposes. Of course, it is the ideal medium for building motor skills and unfurling children's imaginations. As the education wonks tell us, play is the work of children. All this is true, and these aspects of play would probably be better left to take effect on their own rather than be forced along. They are very limited aspects of the expansive power of play.

Play for children, by nature, is pursued until the pleasure runs out. Then it is abruptly ended. Children do not apologize for an exit, they just say, "I don't want to play anymore." Though the differences between play for adults and play for children may look great, especially when comparing tuxedo-clad musicians playing in a concert hall to rope jumpers in a playground, in essence it is very much the same.

What is different about children's play is how naturally they pursue it, and how much time they spend doing it. We need to guard that time as they, and we, grow older. The world, with its addiction to the productive and efficient, allows us little time to play. We must cultivate play not as another item on our to-do list, but as an attitude, requiring not more time, but more wisdom. It takes no more time to put our children to bed playfully than with serious bedtime ritual, because playfulness produces a kind of effluvient energy, and Einstein knew that energy equals time.

I was reluctant to play with my children—not my newborns, not my toddlers, but just around the time they could look expectantly back at me, whether to supply puppet dialogue or lunge at tag. It always seemed a bit undignified, out of character, for me. I definitely had to let something go, a nugget of self-pride, to let myself be led around by my children in play. But letting go turned out to be the best way—and my own rescue out of stodginess. Family is *the* place to be silly, you find out there is life after high school.

What happens when we let our children lead us into play, when we deign to get down on the floor, to get out of the house, to say yes, to squeal? Certainly it changes us, changes the balance of our relationship with our kids. It's nice to be a bit unpredictable with my children—they don't as yet exactly know what I'll say no to, or, even better, yes to.

My kids, right now ten and eight, ask each other, "Wanna play teenagers?" and I feel the hair on my arms quiver a little. "Spare me double purgatory," I pray in a whisper. What exactly does *play teenagers* mean, I wonder? I asked once. "Oh, we do crazy things, it's hard to explain," my oldest offered. "We do a game, we kinda just do things, because we don't really know what teenagers do, but it's really fun. We mostly just goof off with each other, but you have to make sure to act real silly." This is not too bad, I decide. I sigh in relief. I consider asking my husband later if he wants to play teenagers. And I fully intend to draw on my expertise.

I admit, too, I've secretly tape-recorded my kids playing, pretending. I highly recommend it—not as a spying device, but to discover how well formed children's pretend worlds are, and how "big" they are in them. What always surprises me most, beyond the amazingly inventive dramas, worlds, scenarios, skits, and universal productions, is their expectant turn-taking, which they negotiate more fiercely than would Hollywood agents. But they are completely present to each other, not in their usual siblingship, but as the characters they play. It is very different from play alongside each other, where they scrap for territory, bicker over paintbrushes, and generally whine about each other's existence. Play together has its own rules and creates its own order. Each player has to be completely in the game or it fails. In this way playing together builds the relationship between and knowledge of each other. Playing together is a form of true companionship. Sibling play is where they will make the most lasting and memorable life with one another, and if my kids are in a good session I would no more dream of interrupting it for dinner than I would a Board of Trustees meeting.

A friend of mine and his brother, once picture-perfect young boys—you know, matching haircuts and little ties, growing up in a fairly strict home—used to make their fingers into puppets and talk to each other in very sassy voices. They invented a universe of characters who, much to their parents' chagrin and amusement, followed them through high school, college, and into adulthood, even though developmental texts tell you this will not happen.

The two are now separated by three thousand miles, but if one calls when I'm visiting, I always know who it is. My friend, still the tie-wearing, buffed, and reserved gentleman, on finding out it is his brother calling, rushes to the phone and speaks in a funny voice. For the first few minutes of their conversation, their characters appear and squawk away. My friend, every hair smoothed in place, waves his finger puppet next to the receiver as they talk. What began as a silly way of occupying themselves on long car trips as kids comes back to amuse and bless their bond. Play's amusements, begun as children, can last a very long time.

FAMILY PLAY

Family play overturns even Tolstoy, who claimed that all happy families resemble one another—not true, for a family's playing style cannot help but be unique. Family play has its own order, rules, and experience of time—so families who make playtime together build a little world just for them, with their own secret identities and amusements. A family's own style of play builds unity from within; it's not really available to anyone else, pity all the future in-laws.

One family told us of a new game in their lives—a variation of peekaboo for the preteen set. They play spy while shopping. Someone shouts out "Spy" and they scatter among the sales racks and shoe bins, slinking around like earnest secret agents, dashing across aisles not to be seen. It's a nice diversion while buying school clothes.

Family play is not quite as ready to erupt as play with just a partner, or between children. Family play must be seized and shaken a little more. Still, it should be a regular guest at your home and be welcome even when the place is not respectably clean. Leave the clothes to get wrinkled in the dryer; get out to the park with a Frisbee, chocolate, and pears. Let its pleasure happen when it rears its curly-haired head, unscheduled, and resist not. Play is your reward, in the same way a glass of cold lemonade is during an afternoon of housepainting. You would never say, "No, thank you, not right now."

Birthday parties are a perfect place to play. A family I admire gave The Daddy a birthday gift of performing a circus for him, each child making up an animal act and costume. But we don't have to wait for that once-a-year event—cooking together, playing music together, gardening together, fishing. All can produce moments of play if we are looking to grab it—or make it.

A father took his college-age sons away for a week of fishing off a rented houseboat. Imagine the unending jokes when they determined that Dad didn't know how to drive the boat, balanced out only when the sons discovered they didn't really know how to fish. "The best time we ever had with one another," doth sayeth them all.

We can't give up playing with our children, no matter what their age, or ours. While work so often separates us, play unites and reunites. It builds up our family life, family identity, family culture, and can be drawn on all the way through the span of our lives together. Once played, a game or incident endures as a newfound creation of the mind, a treasure to be retained by memory. It is transmitted, and then becomes tradition. It can be repeated at any time; whether it's child's play or a game of chess, its faculty of repetition is like a refrain, sung through a lifetime.

THE COLOR OF PLAY

Play is as necessary to one's life as food. Sam, who died at fifty-three, was remembered at his funeral for many different characteristics and incidents. However, there was one thing that all the mourners at his service together recalled: Sam's love of balloons. They went out of my life when my brothers got too old to throw water balloons at my girlfriends and me. I wanted nothing more to do with them and barely acquiesced to having them at my children's birthday parties. However, for Sam, balloons were a way of life. He always brought a few to parties, blew them up, and surreptitiously dropped them in corners and unoccupied rooms. He would creak open the door of his apartment and float them out to the hallway of his apartment house. No special occasion. He didn't even wait around to see how people reacted—though, usually, the balloons sparked some form of play, they especially loosened tension in the elevators. They got the world around him into a more playful spirit. Everyone noticed one final balloon still lingered in the stairwell of his apartment building the week after his funeral.

Play keeps us attached to the sacred, the imaginary, the human. We grow bigger, become larger entities, in the act of play. We become creators more than creatures. Play, with its mirth and fun, its own inner intensity and tensions, has a profoundly aesthetic quality, despite the potential mess it can leave behind. Play permeates language, ritual, myth, worship, and drama. These great instinctive forces of civilized life are all rooted in the primeval soil of play. And yet, genuine pure play is light and fanciful—a paradise, a feast. To be complete we can't help but play, and play leaves no room for a play-agnostic. A doubter can never really be fully in a game and therefore can't experience the freedom, the expansiveness, the elation, of play. To play one must, at least momentarily, cast doubt, reservation, inhibition, away. For a child this is easy; for an adult it can be excruciating, but we can start small; you don't have to wear a rubber nose to experience the release of play, or pay for a two-week workshop in drama therapy. And don't wait for someone to entertain you. You start. A thrift store can disgorge riches of play objects—let's face it, anything left over from the 1970s is funny. If you see those platform shoes, spend the $2.50. You will find a day to use them.

Be ye as little children—play is a time within time, a time infusing imagination into everyday reality. Chances to run with your children will happen for a very short time in your family life, but play can keep changing, evolving, and injecting new life into today and the years ahead. It is as vital as oxygen. Without it we are living in black and white instead of color.

Three

Family and Spirituality

*S*pirituality in family life starts with heroism, and you star. I have a story that happened with my son. Luca was four, and we were strolling along a big-city street, shopping, stopping, gazing, chatting. We noticed a frail, elderly woman, tottering along in the heat, but stubbornly wearing elegant gloves. We slowly became aware that someone else was watching her, too, eyeing her handbag. It became obvious that he was going to make a dash for it at the first opportunity. I quickly squatted down and explained to Luca what was happening.

"Look, I think that man is going to try to steal that lady's purse. Let's go over and pretend the lady is our grandmother. Maybe he'll go away if he sees she's not alone."

With wide eyes, he agreed. We joined her, I on one side and Luca on the other, walking alongside her at her painfully slow gate, acting as if we were her dearly beloved. She eyed us with suspicion, but stoically kept on, looking straight ahead. She tried to hurry herself up a little. We couldn't explain what we were doing for fear of frightening her; but we stuck it out, chatting about who-knows-what. Luca, I think, told her what he was doing in school. We escorted her, not far, to a bus stop, and waved cheerily good-bye as she boarded, no doubt glad to be rid of us. I turned to Luca in the cloud of the bus fumes, and I will never forget his expression. He was deeply, heroically proud of me. And himself. "We did it, Mommy."

A chapter about family spirituality, you would think, is about how to raise children with respect to religious traditions. It is, and we will come to it. Yet family spirituality is different from religious affiliation. Little has been written about the vital interior space of spirituality among family members. Spirituality in this space is deeply personal and shows who we are. It is not morality—that has more to do with how we treat others in our public life. It is not a rite or a lesson, but a life. Living a heroic life means to give our living, spiritual presence to our families. Spirituality means being informed by the spirit of God and speaks of the reality of a spiritual world. To live not in denial of the material, but in cooperation with it, not in denial of the intellectual, the rational, but in conjunction with it. To be spiritual is not to hole up in retreat, but to go out into the world and explore it, looking there, where God promises to be found. And we go forth a tribe of families, wanting to be heroes to God, heroes to each other. Children especially want to be heroes. Heroism is resisting what is wrong, what went wrong, and working with God to restore good. I'm not speaking here of working in soup kitchens. This heroism is inside family.

Heroism doesn't necessarily require putting oneself in

physical danger. When my friend Chris was a child, his father managed a successful furniture business that was owned by his father-in-law, Gus. Chris's father was in line to inherit the business. Gus was a wealthy man who, through his money, became the patriarch of the extended family. He was a big spender when he wanted to be, and all of his children and their spouses were hoping for a piece of his estate after he died. No one ever crossed Gus or disagreed with him about politics.

Gus, however, was a bigot, and when the family gathered for Sunday dinner a few days after Martin Luther King died, Gus began raving and ranting about how "King had gotten what he deserved." No one dared argue and the silence that descended over the table after Gus had finished his ugly harangue was paralyzing. That's when Chris's father pushed his chair back from the table, with the entire family watching—his own children, Gus's sons and daughters, and their children—and told Gus, in as diplomatic terms as possible, that he was wrong, that the Reverend King had done much to serve the entire nation. The silence that followed this response was more deadening than the previous one. Gus's eyes filled with venom—no one contested his view on politics—but he said nothing and went back to his supper. When Gus died a few years later, the business went to his ne'er-do-well son, who drove it into the ground. Chris's family paid a price for this heroic moment, struggling financially for many years.

Twenty years later, Chris was having a few beers with his father. For the first time, Chris mentioned the incident. His father began crying right there. He was ashamed that his actions had made the family suffer financially. Yet, for Chris, the moment was among the greatest in his father's life. His father had been a hero, and the price the family had paid—no vacations, secondhand bikes, and the like—was nothing compared with the pride Chris had felt, even as an eleven-year-old, the day his father stood up to Gus.

Heroes are also resisters to the cultural context they find themselves in. Every culture offers easy compromises for itself, whether laziness or misanthropic competition, false securities or false sacrifices, fraudulent fame or indifferent ignorance. Perhaps it will come as no surprise to parents with no particular religious affiliation that teaching children to resist the status quo is a spiritual gift; but observing what's wrong about what surrounds us is the first necessary step leading away from the brokenness of a particular culture, setting, or time.

Spiritual leadership at home earns a special place in children's formation, especially in their imagination. Refining our children's spiritual imagination is essential; it will become their storehouse, a granary, for making choices about the way they will face loss or triumph. Their imaginations will be shaped by the world we present them. Children need to hear not only what we believe in, but also what we long for, what we hope for—not just what we think the world *should* look like, but what it *doesn't* look like, and why. And, yes, we want them to be like ourselves, but more. We want our children to admire us on the deepest level of our own spirituality. Not just our ethics, our morality with others, but also what is our being, our nature, what choices we make, who we are in front of the vastness of everyday life, and what we do when confronted with evil. These questions are alive for children from the very beginning of their lives. We cannot wait until we, as adults, as individuals, have finally answered, to our satisfaction, our own questions and doubts about God, the world, and human nature. We are meant to do it together.

We are joined spiritually to our children, it cannot be otherwise. Our children want computer software, Matchbox cars, and Rollerblades. But what they want most from us is *who* we are. To them we are Adam and Eve, the first human specimens of their universe. They keep their eyes on us; they know that no other adult will matter quite so much to them while they grow. They want us to be good. And when we are not good, they watch carefully to see how we will handle ourselves. Here is where most of us will have a chance to be heroic—exactly when we stumble.

Few of us will be presented with classic heroic moments—a car gone brakeless, a neighbor suddenly gone breathless. Our heroism will be extracted from the mush of life. Nevertheless, children, bless them, only need little heroes, but they need them mightily. Our honesty, our vulnerability, before them— as much as is appropriate for their age—is what makes us heroes in their eyes.

When I came home shaken because my professor had roundly chastised me, my daughter stopped playing and came out of her room to see what was wrong. As I spilled out the story of the encounter to my husband, she stood and listened carefully. I had turned in the same paper for two different classes. All along I had an inkling that it was not right to do and that I might get caught, but a pressure-filled semester had sealed my decision to go ahead and hope no one would notice. As the school year progressed, it became clear to me that my integrity as a scholar was out there hanging on the line and I couldn't stand it any longer. I went into his office and simply told him, not trying to excuse or explain myself, just greatly relieved to get what I had done off my chest.

My professor was angry and disappointed. I'm sure he felt duped, because he had taken time to help me develop the paper. My daughter seemed disappointed too. "Well," she sighed, "I wouldn't do that again." She went back to her room to continue playing with her blocks. A short while later she came out again. "It's a good thing you told the truth." She patted me on the shoulder. "What's for dinner?"

The capacity to be a hero, a broken one, a hero out of where we've gone wrong, is a deeply spiritual quality, charted from time immemorial. From Genesis to Greek myths to fairy tales, the theme remains the same: Spiritual identity and spiritual quests lie at the heart of heroic efforts and heroic moments. The story of all these heroisms is not about winning adulation from others. It is about being lost and not knowing what to do, indeed, not knowing even who one is, but finding out through trial. It's about finding a way. And heroes find their way, and themselves, also from time immemorial, not out of their own devices, but by accepting help from some mysterious source. We, too, as parents, need help, and the source may be just as mysterious to us.

We may know "our source" well already, or we may, as new parents, be facing questions about what we believe in that we haven't thought about since high-school religion class or college seminar in philosophy; but raising children brings them all back anew. The moment of birth, the moment you first see that miniature package of perfection, you know you've given birth of the highest order; it's not a watermelon.

Starting from the birth of that new baby, we wonder, "Should we circumcise?" "Should we baptize?" "Are we doing it for them—or for us?" "How can we say anything when we don't yet know what we believe?" "How can I raise my children in a tradition that I had problems with?" "Since my spouse and I disagree, can we avoid this area all together?"

No, you can't. Your children will only make you face these questions later, or, worse, go to some other source to find answers—and don't you want to find your way together, anyway? It helps us, though, to know that this struggle confronts every family. You can take comfort in the fact that other parents—yes, even those who are dragging themselves out of bed for Sunday School—are asking the same questions.

How do you begin? What one needs foremost is courage, for it is dangerous to want to be spiritual. It is a risk to seek: all heroes know this, the fallen ones most of all. To hold off seeking life's answers is a safe, and ultimately, lazy place to live. Love in this place can never be very deep. It cannot hold or heal those experiencing fear, suffering, and pain, as our children surely will. Once we have children, we need to start offering answers, even if they are small ones. To be spiritual means that one wants to know. The point is to try to find out, to keep finding out, to keep looking with one's family. Perhaps some of the answers will even come from them. Whatever those answers will be, they will be formed out of the unique response you've made together to the circumstances of your own family life.

Family spiritual life has a progression, in the same way infants develop their musculature in a certain order, from the neck downward, until they walk. I cannot tell you what you should do, but I can describe some of the essential, universal elements that are necessary and how to acquire these together as a family, until you, too, can begin to walk.

I have, as an anthropologist and a person of faith, had to face many uncomfortable, challenging, and painful questions about expressions of religion, and issues of belief (two different domains). Indeed, as a young college student, I would rather have taken art, but I thought if my faith could survive an academic discipline like anthropology, then I really had something I could live with. I still have many serious questions, which affect the way I live, what I wish to teach my children, how I want to live out my commitments. I have been unable to take the easy way out by saying that every form of religion, every ritual, is saying the same thing. I know they are not. But some things I do know now, not only through faith, but through scholarship, and that is a wonderful gift. Those things I am writing about here.

The universal elements of spirituality are giving our children a relationship with nature; cultivating in them the capacity to observe; honing their ability to listen; helping them create something out of what they have seen and heard; and, finally, showing them how to respond with gratitude for what they have experienced. These capacities are found in all spiritual development, no matter the culture, time, or place.

These universal elements rest on a foundation: that there is a Creator who made good things, however much we have mucked them up along the way, and that we can always get back to the essential good of things, no matter where we find ourselves. There is a well-known story of an Auschwitz survivor, who gave his explanation for enduring as simply this: As a child he heard his mother sing while she did the laundry. Her singing assured him that good existed. He took that with him, he held on to it. All singers know that they have to put into their compositions the bitter part of life as well as the beautiful. When we look, we, too, will see the bitter, the cruel, and so will our children, and that is when we want to hover near them, even after we are gone, a voice still present to them assuring them that there is good in life. Our attitudes and actions will enable our children to know that good does exist. They will need this assurance in the face of life's struggles, and they also will need to know how to get to it themselves. This gives our children a spiritual perspective wholly apart from institutionalized religion. As families, we need our spiritual life not so much on the seventh day, but during the other six days of the week.

HELPING YOUR CHILDREN DEVELOP A RELATIONSHIP WITH NATURE

My father was a child his whole life. It was he who gave me a profound love of nature. The act of turning over a rock seemed, with him, the greatest adventure. Simply by following him on country walks as he pointed out milkweed pods, empty nests, and hidden bugs, I understood that they were important. These things, apart from a life of their own, pointed to the nature of creation, pointed to a Creator. I have an enduring memory of being taken, as a whimpering toddler, to our big picture window slashed by a wild summer storm. My father stood up close to the pane, holding me in his arms. I recall the feeling of the storm as if it were coming directly at me, but also of being elevated and held. The thunder, and especially the lightning, terrorized, but thrilled me too. He taught me to both appreciate the thrill and respect the force, murmuring, "It's wonderful, don't be afraid. I'm here with you," each time a charged flash and crashing boom would explode. "It's something big," he would say.

Albert Einstein recognized the meaning of this force, this "something big," as a three-year-old when, playing with a compass, he understood suddenly that "something deeply hidden had to be behind things." Einstein found this out not because he was a genius, but because he was a child. He kept a child's point of view his whole life. To be a child in nature, no matter your age, you can't help but be spiritually alive, attuned to deeper mysteries, deeper beauties, and terrors that are mostly screened by the modern life we live. As a culture we do not live an existence open to the world, but one that is shielded, sanitized, and protected by plastic wrap.

I have struggled, living smack in the middle of New York City, to give my children a relationship with the natural world, the way my father created one for me. I thought that would mean moving to, if not the little house on the prairie, at least a place with a pocket lawn. Slowly I realized that I didn't need to live in the woods, but only to witness a summer storm unfold on our city stoop, because rain falls everywhere and on everyone.

Since we don't live in the country, we sent away for an ant farm. Remember those funny little kits where you send away for frozen ants? Oh, the day they arrived! The agitation at our mailbox affected even our postman. We tore into the small padded package and out slipped a red-capped vial of suspended ants, about two dozen of them. Did you know that freeze-dried ants assume the fetal position? We shook them into the casement frame made of two panes of glass held about a quarter inch apart. Once those ants warmed up, the sand pressed in between became a marvel of tunnels and mazes. We fed them bits of apple and lettuce. We gave them water with an eyedropper. Under such scrutiny, the sheer excitement of ants is impossible to hide. They don't say God is in the details for nothing. We watched and watched those ants. Their activity provided us with another experience at the window of life. Those ants, in their time, all died, and did *that* lead to a spiritual discussion. We discussed living on a human level compared with that of animals and insects; we discussed the simple possibility that dying as an ant and dying as a human could be different things. The stage was set by nature, and these conversations were waiting for us to activate them to express our doubts, hopes, longings.

We've had some pretty profound exchanges, too, over peonies, a blazing match, and the mystery of a glass of water. To seek out nature, even under glass, leads to wonder, humility, and profound pleasure. These experiences are a first step toward a spiritual perspective, toward beginning to recognize the power, the *good,* of life.

There is one more important thing to say. Nature, and the world in general, is both a good and dangerous place. The dangers we face are not the hurricanes, the droughts, or floods, but teenage suicide, lifelong alienation from the very ones who bore us, profound cynicism. Our cultural environment is far more fatal to us, to our children's wholeness, than the natural one. There is no perfect culture, no perfected society, anywhere, even those closest to nature. We can't run away to Tahiti. And chances are we won't move to that self-sustaining little farm in Vermont. Even if we did, our children would eventually want to escape it and go out into the wide world. The weapons, the tools they will have, they will get from us. The only weapons we have are spiritual ones. Spiritual growth is not a nice feature to enhance our family life in general, like upgrading a hotel room. It is the very foundation on which we build our courage, our love, our survival. To start is very, very simple. Read stories to your children. From Bible stories to Tolstoy, to Isaac Bashevis Singer, you can't help but bring the spirit of life, the struggle for heroism, right inside your door.

Robert Coles, the Harvard psychiatrist, writes in *The Spiritual Life of Children,* "It should come as no surprise that the stories of Adam and Eve, Abraham and Isaac, Noah and the Ark, Abel and Cain, Samson and Delilah, David and Goliath, get linked in the minds of millions of children to their own personal stories as they explore the nature of sexuality and regard with awe, envy, or anger the power of their parents, as they wonder how solid and lasting their world is, as they struggle with brothers and sisters, as they imagine themselves as actual or potential lovers, or as actual or potential antagonists. The stories are not mere symbolism, giving expression to what people go through emotionally. Rather, I hear children embracing religious stories because they are quite literally inspiring—exciting their minds to further thought and fantasy and helping them become more grown, more contemplative and sure of themselves." These stories, he shows, "have a way of being used by children to look inward as well as upward." And they do not stop having their way with us as we grow into adults.

THE CAPACITY TO OBSERVE

We were born to look around. It is not a small feat. As author Elizabeth Balliett Platt notes, "Eyesight leads to insight." We need our eyes for wisdom. Patient observation makes us wonder why things look the way they do. Among our family's favorite stories is *The Giver,* by Lois Lowry, which tells of a society perfectly planned and ordered. In order to achieve this perfect peace, perfect calm, the people had to give up seeing things in color. For generations, as far back as anyone can remember, no one has seen any color, just gray, black, and white. Even death is simply a gray thing—as is love. Until one little boy comes along; he discovers that seeing color creates passionate attachments, and this passion is disruptive. His story is about finding abundant love again through the struggle to look, to know, through understanding the complexity of things.

The spiritual skill of looking starts not with understanding a unified whole, but with taking things apart. Every child does this instinctively. "Hey!" you hear from down the hallway. "This thing comes apart!" And there, strewn about on the floor, sits grandfather's pocket watch. My brothers dismantled dozens of transistor radios, often without permission of the owner. My husband, at the age of eight, shed tears over his dead goldfish and then promptly asked his father if he could dissect it.

We are natural-born scientists, interested in breaking things down into their constituent parts. By studying their color, shape, texture, and composition, we make our deepest discoveries, gain our best comprehension. Our children already know this, but they need help refining this skill. If we encourage them to value this skill, they will take it with them, improve upon it to keep seeing, keep knowing. While these observational powers will no doubt pay off in school, they will yield greater dividends as our children embark on the search for meaning—a voyage that will be definitive to their happiness.

Bringing this developed capacity into everyday life is important to our children's spirituality, but we also need to practice it as families. Studying things together, whether it's how the garden grows, or turning over that rock, or analyzing a painting or piece of music, builds up our common appreciation of life. We can see when a family walks down the street as disparate individuals rather than as a whole. Dad leads the bunch, hurrying everyone along to some store. Behind him are two children, rehashing the argument de jour. Then comes Mom, trying like a sheepherder to keep the jumble together. Last but not least is the youngest child, moping about how everyone walks too fast for him. The effect is quite different when we make an effort to walk together, to share one conversation, an exchange of observations about street life by each family member. It can truly be spiritual—indeed, it's a form of congregate discovery. We will have our days, of course, hurrying everyone along, but let's have our days of looking together too.

THE ABILITY TO LISTEN

Spiritual listening is, quite simply, eavesdropping on life. A few years ago, on a rainy Saturday afternoon, my daughter and her friend were driving me berserk with their bickering. With two hours to go until the girl's mother arrived to pick her up, I called the girls into the kitchen to make cookies. "That's for five-year-olds," they said to me. I sent them off and they started fighting again, this time with one imitating the voice of the other. I was quite impressed; they'd been friends for some time and had each other's intonations down to a T. I decided to take advantage of the situation. I threw some potato chips into a bowl and called them back into the kitchen.

"You girls can really imitate each other," I said, pouring two glasses of soda. "Let's hear some more."

They looked at me with puzzlement.

I explained. "Let me hear you do your teacher."

This they gladly did, and with an accuracy that would have gotten them sent to the principal's office had they done it in school.

The game began to work. My daughter imitated a clerk who works behind the counter at a local deli. She had his gestures and his Brooklyn accent down cold. Her friend did a great imitation of her older sister whining about boyfriends. They were doing imitations not to mock, but because they had really paid attention, really listened and enjoyed the character, facial gestures, and passions of the people they were parroting.

Here are children who had been studying the world. Nothing was lost on them. We need this attitude, and we need to nurture it further as families.

We are always listening, but so much of life passes us by like a radio left on while we do the bills. To truly listen one has to be still, attentive, open, cocked. We have to turn off the voices in our head, to give up our inward preoccupations, and listen to the outside world. What exactly are we listening for? A snatch of conversation caught at a coffee shop or on a checkout line can reveal so much about the richness of life. It gives us a perspective on the frail humanness in which we are each encased. Besides, eavesdropping is a secret ticket to free humor.

Some dear friends, Karen and Will, tell and retell a story reflecting this. Will's mother, Betsy, had come to town for a visit. Before coming up to their apartment, she stopped at a coffee shop across town for a bite to eat. As she sipped her coffee slowly, she inspected her fellow diners. It was a quiet afternoon period when the regulars came in. A dapper elderly gentleman appeared, definitively took a seat at the counter, elegantly adjusted his cuffs, his tie, his napkin, and began ordering. Though she never caught a glimpse of his face, she could hear him quite clearly.

He wanted a bagel, cream cheese, and sardines, and a cup of tea. Betsy noticed that as each dish appeared, he would send it back. "Could you cut the cream cheese in a triangle, please?" he asked the counterman. "This bagel is not hot enough." "May I have a pickle on the side?" "There are three sardines here. I'd like four." She listened with amusement, taking pleasure in the sweet comedy of it all, and her delight grew as she noted that the counterman accommodated each request without flinching.

Having had the meal exactly as he wished, the man ate, regally stood, and demanded the bill. "By the way," he called out as the counterman tore off his tab, "I also need a take-out order for my wife. A blueberry muffin, if you please."

The counterman obligingly handed him a paper bag. The man looked inside and said, "This is a bran muffin."

"Your wife doesn't like the blueberry."

Naturally, Betsy couldn't wait to relate this tale to Karen and Will. When she finally arrived at their apartment she told the story over dinner, relishing each detail. When she finished Karen sat quietly in her chair for a few moments, and then asked, "Where was this coffee shop?" Betsy gave the location. "And was this man wearing a gray fedora?" Karen asked. Betsy affirmed the detail. "Oh," Karen said, "that was my grandfather. He always orders that way."

SPIRIT AND IMAGINATION

This anecdote illustrates more than a charming, entertaining incident, besides noting that we're all related in some mysterious way. When you overhear all the little specificities that make up someone's daily life, you may react in one of two ways: with a sense of empathy or with derisive indifference, a dismissal. To be tied to life, we have to care, to observe, and to listen. It is the myriad of particulars that define a person, like Karen's grandfather, and touch us with their uniqueness and divine quirkiness. We become aware of how frail we are, yet how miraculous—how close to vulnerability we live, how dependent we are on one another to hang on to life. Nevertheless, we persist, and endure in our own indefatigable individuality. This is the art of inspired spiritual listening that changes us and our family. This kind of listening entails an exchange of place, an act of imagination, to be able to put oneself in the other's shoes. It is why spirituality and the imagination are so closely tied together, each being in the service of the other. It is why so often reading great novels is a spiritual experience, because we have been with the hero, lived out the story through his or her eyes. This capacity allows us to enlarge our experience, to go out into the world in many ways, and no way is more enhancing or exciting than through childlike imagination. To dismiss another is to always be bounded by oneself, to be one's own god alone and not find God in others. Imagining is a spiritual act at its essence. To imagine is at the height of our own divinity. Made out of the imagination of God, as we are, we are Godlike when we imagine.

Imagination is necessary for spiritual growth, not because we "make it up" but because we are able to imagine more of reality, reality that is otherwise inaccessible. Imagination is our own interior cosmoscope. We don't throw out our senses with imagination, we open and refine them to their fuller capacities. Every description of the spirit involves stretching our imagination, trying to grasp it in ways that are new and heretofore "unimaginable," unimagined. The first spiritual question we all ask is one derived not from what we see, but what we don't see. "Where do we come from?" We theorize about this—*theory* derived from the Latin, meaning "to look at by a mental viewing, a pictured contemplation"—and the theories we begin to chew on require our best imagination. We put imagination to work immediately, naturally. Author Robert Coles's report of children hearing the voice of God describes their struggle to explain that while, yes, they do imagine it, it is real. "It's like imagination, but not made up, not like a dream, it's real," they insist again and again. They resort to imagery to attempt an accurate description for their impaired listener. Imagery, viewing by imagination, is a visual, sensual, and interior language trying to describe a reality that cannot be described by one language alone. Yet how do we use imagination without lurching into craziness? One thing we can know is that true imagination leads us into more possession of ourselves, not less.

There is outside listening: the eavesdropping, the hearing conversations, hearing music, hearing each other; and then there is inside listening. Much has been written about contemplation, about silence and spirituality, but it is written for adults. Yet we have a role as parents to help our children discover and develop their own inner life, their own spiritual imagination, and match it with the reality they encounter. The first task is to remove the maze of obstacles that our culture places in their way. The earnest efforts we make to keep our children from being bored, to keep them learning, happy, and occupied, can stand in the way of the growth of their spirituality, which is the only way to deeper knowledge, happiness, and vocation. The simple act of providing times of silence in your home can come not only as a relief from the din, but also as times of peace, prayer, and discovery. This will become more difficult, but more urgent, as they grow older, as they outgrow the natural times of imaginary exploration and curious wonderings they engaged in as younger children. Older children are even more inundated with noise and voices from every direction.

Our second task will be to tell them silent listening is a legitimate way to respond to life's ills. They must have some idea that listening is even a possibility, an experience waiting for them. Contemplation is a gift, but we must open the package. Without this, they won't have much chance to develop a spiritual life in a material world. What exactly are we helping our children to listen for? For the spirit of life, which leads us, consoles us, blesses us, and calls us deeper into life.

One boy interviewed by Coles explained that the voice he heard was like no other he knew of. It wasn't his father's voice, the boy stated, it wasn't his mom's voice, either, because he heard things they would never say. It wasn't even his own voice, he clarified, because he could never have thought these things up. "When I hear God talking, I realize He's different, lots different. I don't hear people talk like Him. . . . I'm not sure God's perspective is my dad's or mine. Our God worries about us down here. . . . He sees all the trouble here, and he must be sad. When I pray, I ask God to help me. I think I'm trying to find out what is the 'best,' by asking Him." This from an eleven-year-old.

The toughest part of silent listening is the waiting that goes with it. We have to wait exactly because we have not found all the answers, they are still coming in. But if waiting is hard work, it can also serve as a kind of rest, a kind of in-between from our cares. Even God took rest, and God knows we need it.

Why do we look, what are we listening for? The finest minds, and there have been many, have thought about these questions. They all have noted one thing in common: what is spiritual, what is divine, reveals itself. We can't force it, but we can wait for it, watch for it—we can learn how to spot it. And why should we want to do that? Because we are not just physical bodies, physical families, we are spiritual families too. We live in a reality that is not only ordinary, but extraordinary. When this extraordinary reality shows itself in those moments of insight and awe, we respond, we are stricken with how miraculous life is. Remember when that newborn was first placed in our arms? We want to respond. It is this spirit of response that we want to keep open. It is this spirit in our families that will see us through all the changes, loss, and grief we will have to face. This Spirit, too, is what will keep us together even as we pass from life.

Indeed, the miraculous, the sacred, is something that shows itself, but only momentarily. Not only must we train ourselves to look and be willing to recognize and employ a sacred moment when it shows itself, we must also be willing to let it go and not try to capture, cement, or solidify it for our safety's sake. To do so is to violate its essential nature and what it does reveal to us, which is that we must live for many stretches in the dark. We must live from one rope swing to the next. Not only must we be willing to recognize that moment but have the faith to let go, to trust the next moment will arrive, it awaits us. We must be looking forward to the next time when the sacred will show itself to us. This is how one lives a life of faith, looking for the sacred, inviting it in, making a place for it. A life lived this way is an act of faith.

CREATING AS A SPIRITUAL ELEMENT

If a fundamental step toward a spiritual life is to take things apart, the next step is putting things together again, but in a new way. Creating is a spiritual skill because it brings something new into being. We are emulating the Creator. For children, this is very exciting, even if the creation is a necklace made of dental floss and dried rigatoni. If we are ready to admit that drawing, writing, singing, et cetera, is a kind of self-expression, the next step is to see creating also as the divine expression that it is. Even the smallest act is a spiritual gesture, a deeply human gesture. Through the work of our hands, we pour ourselves into life.

Those who put things back together inspire our admiration, especially musicians and artists and, if we're enlightened, the dishwasher repairman. We recognize and appreciate that they are doing something spiritual, confirmed by that rush of gratitude we feel when the work is finished. It's the process itself that is a spiritual skill, even though we tend to associate creating more with a fine end-product. We're told we have to make something extraordinary to be officially labeled creative. But, we can't leave creating solely to artisans or artists, if we want to have a spiritual life. We are born with the urge to create and we have to find a way to keep it growing, both in our children and ourselves. We wouldn't dream of dropping out at the third grade, nor should we drop out of our spiritual education.

Polly Berrien Berends, author of *Gently Lead: How to Teach Your Children About God While Finding Out for Yourself,* asked a class of fourth graders if there were any artists among them. Only a few raised their hands. That's crazy. Though some students show true proclivity at drawing, every one of them is creative right down to the end of their shoelaces, and every parent knows this. Secretly we all suspect we've given birth to the next Picasso. We're all creative, we just get talked out of showing it, we are all artists of our own gifts. We recognize it more in little children, who have not yet learned to be limited by the world's definition of "art." We have to recapture a larger working definition of creativity, and spirituality, too, one that reflects our whole essence, even if that essence is busy bustling the house back together again.

How do we amplify this natural creativity in a setting that undermines it? First we communicate to our children that, of course, they are creative, but then we give them lots of opportunities to practice an expanded definition. Cooking, making paper books, mud pies, making and bringing ice tea to the lonely neighbor—things that require energy and action and get-out-of-the-chair. All creativity requires work. But this kind of work is a welcome relief from the stunning lethargy created by endless television, computer games, and the just-distract-me-from-my-boredom inertia. Creating anything allows epiphanies in.

There are different kinds of putting-things-back-together-again, all of them creative. There is the kind where we are restoring and reassembling what we've observed and heard, having mastered how their parts fit together; with it comes an understanding. That's the clock-tinkering kind—the learning-French kind, the educational, scientific kind. Then there is the kind where we add something new, or combine elements in new ways. That's the throw-it-in-the-soup kind, the improvisational humming kind, the really nice additional touch. And then there is the kind of putting-back-together-again-that-which-is-broken. Among children you need that kind every day. Restoring, healing, is the most profound kind of putting-back-together-again. Creating is not only to make something new, but to make something complete unto itself—newly whole, even if still showing its dents, dings, and chips.

We have a fix-it box in our house, where we throw broken toys, picture frames, gadgets that need tinkering. I keep the glue bottle and a pair of pliers right in the box. Some days, when the kids are bored, I suggest getting out the "it's broken" box, which usually leads to a certain amount of frustration when the glue won't hold, or it becomes clear that an item cannot really be repaired. But just as often it leads to a couple of hours' tinkering, with a triumphant hurrah at the end. Besides, I feel a secret kind of pleasure when I find a little bed, made out of paper towels, under the kitchen table, holding a plastic animal with its torn leg carefully but childishly taped. It can be more redemptive, more fulfilling, to repair and heal that which has been broken than to possess something that has never been broken at all. There is special power in this idea for stepfamilies. They can never go back and make things as they were, but they can heal their families. They can create something new that, without superseding that earlier life, goes in an entirely different direction. Creating new times together, new projects together, new memories, repairs old wounds, which leave their scars but which we can heal by creating new, different experiences, relationships, ideas.

An episode dear to me about spiritual discovery involves a wounded, very intelligent young man, a beauty in his prime, backpacking through Europe right after his graduation. He was really running from his busted-up family. He stopped off with a friend of ours in a tiny hamlet in Switzerland, high on a mountain road, the cliffs covered with moss and ferns and ancient trees. Our friend took him for many long walks along this road, listening and discussing his life, trying to lead him to a deeper perspective. One day, during a particularly painful conversation, our young man had a spiritual epiphany. In a flash of insight he suddenly saw all that had happened to him and in his family life not as the series of arbitrary incidents, erratic occurrences, capricious events, lost attempts he had feared them to be, but as a whole, a story of his life that he could lead on somewhere.

He didn't cry, "I found the answer!" He didn't scream, "I can be happy now!" He ran down the road shouting, "It's together! It is together!"

How can *It is together!* be a spiritual answer, a spiritual response? Spirituality is precisely different from morality, because morality is us in relation to others. Spirituality is our relationship with God. Spirituality is not some New Age thing dunked in an herbal brew, but very real grappling with God. It is about what we do, in God's presence, about what others have done to us. To bring that together—God's presence with our history of others, our future with others—is first spiritual, later moral. Putting things back together again is not just an expression for restoration, but recognition that we live among broken things, including broken relationships, and that is where family spirituality comes in. It is the salve to the busting-up life delivers us every day. It is more than psychological clarity. Knowing, psychologically, what is the problem is not enough; we have to put it together with what to do next. Spiritual growth comes from creating the next step. We continually create our relationships. We can never take our relationships with our children, or our parents, for granted. They have to be made into the story of our life, each day; a narrative created, creatively, out of the little pieces of the day. It's a lot of work, but the product is fabulous.

Responding with Gratitude

We don't generally associate gratefulness with sharp criticism, but they are from the same family. Responding with gratitude is the result of being truly critical, judging and assessing with a careful eye. Once we observe, once we listen, we can make important distinctions, to assess and critique the world around us. Gratitude is the natural response for understanding those differences.

If we teach our children to spot the good in life, through enhancing their abilities to see it, to hear it, they will respond naturally with awareness, acknowledgment, and appreciation. These abilities are the very same ones necessary to spot what is shallow, cheap, or evil. These critical faculties are always urgently needed, but more so today, inundated as we are with the flattened perspective of featureless television and films, consumerized emotions, and the pursuit of high excitement at all cost. Boredom and titillation are our culture's version of indifference.

This indifference comes precisely from an inability to comprehend the difference between things—good things and bad things—an inability to understand distinctions between levels of value. Ignorance of the magic of unfolding life is lost in our revved-up, shoot-'em-up, hit-the-button society. Ignorance is the opposite of gratitude, whereas critical assessment leads us there.

Responding with gratitude is a very distinct kind of pleasure in life, a commingling of complex emotions and realizations that comes only after a line of reasoning is exhausted. The endless *whys* a preschooler asks you are an attempt to reach a place of relief—for both parties. The satisfaction of comprehending the relation between A and B results in gratitude. As simple as it seems, as humble and serflike, gratitude is a sophisticated, intellectual response requiring understanding and new-found apprehension.

And children are the best practitioners of both gratitude and humility because they are so willing to learn, so eager to discover how a magnet works, why a bird sings, why leaves change color. But all this is lost, slowly drained, as children encounter the broken, the fallen, the disappointments of living, unless we've given them the skills to renew and repair themselves, to challenge life back. Humility and gratitude will not come from our educational institutions or from our marketplace life. That's why we need to live a spiritual life together, under our own roof.

These universal elements, to be in touch with the natural, divinely created world, to look, to listen, to create, to respond—these capacities, once gained, always remain. But they are much harder to acquire as adults and may not form at all if we do not cultivate them for our children. The developed capacity to critique the world, with a spiritual eye, to separate the wheat from the chaff, is urgently needed in our current environment of astonishing materialism, egoism, shallowness, and indifference that surrounds our children. How else do we do that? Children can also point the way.

CHILD-LED SPIRITUALITY

While we lead our children in spirituality, they, too, can lead us. Even though we cultivate all these elements for our children, we are not completely responsible for our children's spirituality. They come preloaded. There is a story that circulates about a little boy who begs his parents to let him be alone with their newborn. The parents, mindful of all the tales they've heard about sibling rivalry and handy pillows, are reluctant to leave the boy alone with the baby. He pesters and begs and they even become a bit fearful because he is so intense. They tell him, yes, though Mommy has to stay in the far corner of the room. He insists he has to be alone. Finally, the parents agree, but for their peace of mind they listen in on the nursery intercom. The boy goes in, approaches the crib, and whispers, "Baby, tell me what God looks like, I'm forgetting." Such is the effect of the world on our children, eventually they forget.

Yet while they are children, their imagination of the spiritual is quite possibly more profound than adults'. They certainly make more time for it. As Robert Coles documents in *The Spiritual Life of Children,* they have, in those quiet moments, their preoccupations with life's questions and with its spiritual answers. Coles interviewed children from all over the world, finding that, without question, children lead spiritual lives. They can even illustrate them. He includes the drawings. My favorite thing about these pictures is that many of the children earnestly provide arrows pointing to God. Some days, I need that.

In the same way that the compass for Einstein pointed the

way to some hidden force, children can act as our spiritual compass. They lead us by their attitude, their outlook which is fresh and alive, tender as baby lettuce.

The features of children's spirituality are very distinct, the most striking being the universality of it, regardless of the cultural context or parental point of view. Children everywhere have spiritual yearnings. Coles quotes a young Hopi girl, "The 'spirit' is when you go running for someone. It is when you try to send signals to someone. It is when you are being as much you as you can be." Coles had to finally break out a separate developmental category in his long life of psychiatric work and call it distinctly spiritual.

Children have a strong sense of humility about themselves. It enables them to believe that there is someone big out there who can help them. They are humble about discovery as well. A child's first posture toward the world is "I don't know. I must find out. I must learn how"—an attitude from which we adults can benefit. Children come equipped with a sense of justice, an innate equity. Just try cutting a piece of cake for two children. Sage grandmothers always let *them* divide it. To the crumb, to the crumb, they divvy it in two. Even Solomon didn't cut it this close. Their capacity for judgment, for assessment can be better than Solomon's too. Children will assess an entire situation, counting all the variables, before they make a decision. To witness this, be with them in a toy store at five minutes to closing time.

Children's sense of time is different from adults'. It is elongated because they haven't yet suffered the accumulation of many experiences to detract from the present. They take all the time they need to address what life puts in front of them, in the right-now. They will have to be older before they say,

"Oh, it's the same old thing." However, this is not something you can explain to them on a long car trip.

Children's honesty, their inner integrity, is already in place. My son Luca more than chagrined me, once, after I hung up the phone. I'd declined an unwanted invitation by saying we'd be out of town. He knew perfectly well we were not going anywhere. "Mommy, every time you lie, a little bit of you dies."

Children slowly discover that the world is broken, that people, also, are broken, that things don't always work according to the golden rule. This is when their distinct take on spirituality can offer us the most. They know, with sheer certitude, that we were made to be given and to be received. They know that there is something wrong with the world when we are not abundantly loved. This innate knowledge, a tremendous clue to the universe, comes from children. The outermost line, the boundary of cosmology, is already drawn, that we were made to be loved, we have only to fill in the blank. They insist on humility, justice, fairness, honesty.

As parents we are forced to explain why these things get lost in life. As families engaged in the discussions of life, we work out together what our responses to this loss will be. We needn't expend our energy trying to screen them from brokenness, from the rough world. It's futile, and we will only have wasted all the time we had to strengthen them through spiritual maturity. Instead children's spirituality is a natural springboard toward deeper discussions, a deeper comprehension about what happens when things go wrong. If we are with them when these experiences occur, companions in their experiences, if we are willing to discuss life's disappointments, life's thwarting, to offer comfort and consider questions together, then they will not grow up to be bitter. We cannot shelter them from life, we just need to stay close by their side.

THE FAMILY PRACTICE OF SPIRITUALITY

There are many things we can do to join our children in their spiritual lives and to foster its development. Foremost among them is to take your children's questioning seriously. They are not trying to say cute things for you to squeal over or collect for a scrapbook. They are wrestling with Jacob's angel, the Gordian knot, Descartes's dictum, perhaps more sincerely than Jacob, Gordius, or Descartes. Honor these wonderings for what they are: serious intellectual work. Wonder *with* them.

We can pray in their presence. Offering thanks over meals is a traditional start. I hope you don't stop there. One girl told me of catching her mother closing her exhausted eyes, not for a moment of respite, but for something else, something she recognized immediately as prayer, though her mother never prayed out loud, or with them. This little girl told me she's thought a lot about seeing her mother do this, though she was reluctant to ask her reticent and private mother about it. "Ever try it yourself?" I asked her. "I'm working it in," she replied.

On the street, passing a drugged-out unconscious figure, a mother grabs her children's hands right then and there, huddling together and whispering up a plea for help, peace, grace, upon the unknown body lying there. "Does this really help?" her little boy earnestly asks. "Well, we won't know right away, but we should find out eventually," she reported saying.

We can provide them with time to worship with us, but also with time to worship on their own because children, too, need to worship, and not just get stuck watching the spiritual professionals. A big rock is a good place to sit and worship, looking out at the world. That feeling you feel, when you see the woods, the ocean, a flower, is the first-fruits offering of worship. The natural world, not the man-made world, provides us with the right proportions, the right perspective.

By naming the feeling of awe in the face of nature for your children, you claim worship as a common human experience. We can worship, too, by being a loving, listening family. Children can lead us in worship, often by the very questions they ask. We adults are forced to acknowledge awe at both our bigness and smallness. These moments rarely happen inside the houses of religion, but in our home, or out of doors, on that fabled rock perhaps.

We can read aloud, either from favorite stories or religious texts. The act of reading aloud together is a family communion and is deeply comforting. Books play a special, a unique, role in developing a spiritual life, not only for children, but for adults. Surprisingly it is not only the book's content, but the simple act of reading, which is spiritual. Reading alone tutors children to sit quietly and enter a new world through imagining the place and action of the story. It is a spiritual skill to be able to envision another reality, to conjure up other possiblities, bolstered by a rich store of details from everyday experience. "Isn't it funny that you can make a little picture in your head about things you read? I always know just how to make it look," said my daughter Alma, fingers pressed right to the middle of her forehead.

A book teaches you to be present to the moment, to a

single page, indeed, not to turn the page before it has told all. As the action unfolds, we are there, reading each word, acquiring each detail, because we know we need every sentence to understand the whole story. To what, today, besides reading, do we give this kind of concerted attention? Having an increased attention span, paying true attention, leads us into richer awareness of the seen and unseen.

A book teaches waiting, waiting to have the whole story in front of you before you come to a conclusion, of suspending judgment till the whole tale is in. Waiting, we know, is also a spiritual skill.

Playing musical instruments together is great fun, but also spiritually binding. Surely, music is the first language of spirituality, a divine offering. From tribal drums to a Handel chorus, music pierces us. If we don't play an instrument, or not all family members do, at least we can sing. Singing as a family does not mean emulating the von Trapps. If you are afraid to sing—hum, or get a harmonica. Making up very simple songs about your family is delicious to young children. Your children's sweet, quavering voices will ring in your ears for a very long time. Your music together doesn't have to be on a spiritual text. Singing itself is an act of vulnerability, another way to be with each other, open to each other. And if we can't sing, and won't hum, then we can listen to music together.

Listening to music with our family, any music, is more than entertainment alone. It means we've gone somewhere, journeying across the sounds together. On a particularly rough day my husband will say, "Symphony tonight?" and this is his shorthand for saying that he is so exhausted that all he wants to do is throw himself on our bed, in the dark, at the end of the day, and listen together to our latest favorite music. We come back from floating through a piece of music together renewed.

We "gave" a symphony to each of our children. Like names, these symphonies have become a part of their identity. Alma was Dvořák, Luca was Tchaikovsky. We can't say exactly how we decided which one was for each child. These pieces of music, like the children's names, just seemed to fit. When Carlo was first carried home from the hospital, Beethoven's Ninth was playing on the radio. It was also the last symphony my father heard before he died, four months before Carlo's birth. We knew it was the right one.

We can begin to share a spiritual life with our children at any age. Whether they are tiny or teens, whether they are your children or your stepchildren, whatever your family configuration, all it takes to begin is some honesty on your part. Children, no matter how old, never forsake responding to real conversation and genuine attention. Invite them for a walk, take them to a café. You don't have to extract out of them what they are thinking; instead you can describe your own questions and how you have tried to handle them. Believe it or not, you can tell your children your problems, albeit in a modified way, your struggles with friendship, corruption at work, how you wished you had been with your own parent. You are not telling them to get their advice—though don't be surprised if some of it is terrific—but to share who you are, to show that we all struggle and here's how you do it. A spiritual life with your family is different from simply offering your children advice about life. It is traveling together because you both don't know, and you are finding out together.

COMEDY AS A SPIRITUAL WEAPON

David Denby, a film critic, and a father of boys, nine and thirteen, writes in *The New Yorker*, "We are all in the same boat, afloat in the boundless sea. For both relaxed and authoritarian parents, the real issue is much larger than bad TV shows and movies. (There are always some good ones.) We all believe in 'choice' but our children, to our chagrin, may no longer have the choice *not* to live in pop [culture]. For many of them, pop has become not just a piece of reality—a mass of diversions, either good or bad, brilliant or cruddy—but the very ground of reality. The danger is not mere exposure to occasional violent or prurient images but the acceptance of a degraded environment that devalues everything—a shadow world in which our kids are breathing in an awful lot of poison without knowing that there's clean air and sunshine elsewhere. They are shaped by the media as consumers before they've had a chance to develop their souls." He cites this as the "landscape of the American child." And so it is.

However, families are the first landscape of a child, and therefore we have the powerful advantage of establishing the ground they stand on before they face out to the world. We can give them another reality. Comedy is not often thought of as a great spiritual weapon, but it is. It punctures perfectly the overwrought pleas for purchase, romance with shampoo Cinderellas, and rescue à la air-pumped action figures. "Mommy," a child yells at yet another TV pitch, "a little green man wants me to buy pink cereal! Isn't that funny?" Say yes. Humor provides children with the critical eye that allows them to dissect and defuse images meant to allure. Go ahead and poke fun at pouty-mouthed models, hopelessly posed mannequins, and the seasonally underdressed. It begins to give your child the right idea. They will take it from there.

Comedy could not have existed in Eden. Play, of course, was there, but comedy, no. Comedy is laughing at the misplaced, ironically matching what is with what has been lost; comedy is how we suffer, yet survive.

RENEWING TRADITIONS

If they have a baby, they'll be back in the pew, goes the priestly proverb. But surely we don't want to feel like hooked fish about our religious traditions. Religious traditions have long been a pathway for maintaining profound relationships within the family and across generation lines. But it is often the generation lines, with in-laws and grandparents, where some of the tensest conflicts about this topic are found. How have other families faced this?

A family with old-world grandparents went through tremendous conflict over the baptism of the grandchildren. The parents, thoughtful and thoroughly modern, did not want to have their children baptized as infants, without any memory of the experience, without any personal meaning, without any choice. They wanted their children to develop their own spiritual comprehension first. But the extended family was in conflict. A christening was expected. The uncles cajoled. "Think what you're doing to our mom! You're killing her with this! Just have the kids baptized, for God's sake. . . . If you don't want to do it, just *tell* them you did it, you're driving us all crazy!" The grandfather threatened to take the children and have them baptized when they visited. All the family members couldn't understand this new variation on their sacred tradition.

After a while the parents began to differ. The wife began to question, under all the pressure from her family, why they should alter centuries of practice. The husband remained adamant. Things came to a head by the time the third child was born. They just had to do something. The answer came from the oldest child, now eight. "But I'm ready to be baptized," she stated. The parents seized the moment and decided to take all three children, one eight, one four, one newborn, and have them baptized together, thus creating a different experience for each child. They made the tradition fit their family and also used a different approach with each child.

My neighbors are hip musicians. He's a jazz pianist, she's a songwriter, competent, talented, aswirl in the world of the latest, yet longing for a past too.

Aliza told me, "When we got married we felt we had to start doing the sabbath rituals, now that we had a home of our own. But it was so bizarre, it felt very contrived, inauthentic, at the beginning. But slowly we saw it was like playing the piano, doing the scales, it was the practicing of it that made it slowly come alive, gain depth, accumulate history."

What Aliza had discovered for herself was what sociologists and psychologists are rapidly rewriting into working theories of growth. Maggie Scarf writes in *Intimate Worlds: Life Inside the Family* that insight, growth, and deeper understanding are more likely to develop in the practice of a tradition, an activity, an exercise, than in the thinking of it.

There is a regenerative effect in returning to religious origins, but we have to make them our own, come to terms with them for our own families. Traditions without personal meaning become hollow vessels instead of filled ones. Developing traditions provides another chance for your children to know you, know your particular take on spiritual matters, even if you are facing conflict in your own family. An interfaith couple, Jewish and Christian, made a very personal attempt when over the years they developed the idea of a Passover celebration folded into the family Christmas Eve meal. While their extended families viewed this with reproval, and questioned whether it truly represented either tradition, the parents took refuge in the knowledge that their children had watched them struggle with the differences and aim toward insight rather than doing nothing, or attempting no reconciliation.

Children will relink us with past family traditions. There is great revivifying power in this, but to be authentic, we have to claim it as we need it for our time, our circumstances, our family. Religious institutions are facing the same questions of modernization as your family and they, too, have been engaged in the process of authenticity, relevancy, and change. In returning to your sacred traditions, in seeking out the religious officials of your tradition, you may find they are far more open than you thought. It is possible to start again.

As our family's spiritual life develops, we need to have a communal way to practice it as well. We may forsake a religious tradition entirely and go for working in soup kitchens, or we may need to find a new tradition that has not been our heritage, but in some way, again, made out of our own family circumstances, we will be strengthened by joining with others to profess and share what we've discovered.

THE SECRET HERO

A final thought on parenting and spirituality. You may feel uncomfortable and puzzled about this or you may be the most agnostic person you know, and yet, in loving your children, you are practicing the profoundest spirituality. In this you are heroic, and there are days when you know it. You know you've been stretched to the limit, faced insanity, wept in the closet, physically found an entirely new level of exhaustion. It's called sacrifice. No one else, except maybe, *maybe,* your partner, will ever know what you've done. No one else will ever guess how hard it has been. No one will thank you for it. Even when your children have their children, they will only vaguely realize what you've done—they will be too frantic caring for their own kids. Yet you do it. Now, that's heroism.

Four

The Physical Life of Family

*O*ur bodies are what we first give to each other as families—as husband and wife, in labor, in birth, and what we leave at death.

The priest shook his head when my father, fast dying from cancer, requested immediate cremation and a simple service.

"I can't be cremated?" my father asked.

"Oh, you can be cremated, but first you've got to give them the body."

My father gave him a puzzled look. Was Father Jack talking about donating the organs of an eighty-year-old man? "Give it to *whom?*"

"Your family. After you die, it belongs to them. They get to see it, touch it, bid it farewell, one last time."

My father thought that one over for a long while. He was no sheep of the church. In the end, he agreed, because if there was one thing he learned as his life slipped away, it was how sacred the body was.

I had arrived in the snowbound Michigan north two weeks before he died to be with him and help my mother out. In a sense I got my "daddy" back, except our roles were now reversed. He had bathed me as an infant; I massaged his weakened hands with oil. He had rushed to my bed at two A.M. to dispel bad childhood dreams; I sat by his bedside to give him sips of water all night. After a few days, I placed a call to my husband, saying, "He's not going to make it through another week. I'm going to stay on here to help my mom, okay?"

When I hung up, I found my mother looking pointedly at me. "That won't be necessary," she said. "Your father and I wanted each of you kids to come and say good-bye, but please don't stay any longer, because I want to be the one to care for him. After he's gone I won't be able to do that anymore."

My mother told me that one of the greatest things she would miss in their fifty-one years of marriage, was not their weekly dinners out at country supper clubs or holidays spent around a roaring fire with the family, but simply crawling into bed and sidling up next to him every night. It was simple. She just wanted to lie down next to him, her body length next to his.

In order to cherish the body—both those of others and our own—we must first recognize the inescapable fact that it will one day break down and turn to dust. This should trigger a certain urgency in us to care for one another's arms, feet, and face and to enjoy each and every stage a body passes through on its journey from birth to death.

A body is not just housing for the soul; it, too, is sacred.

Our body is the instrument of our spirituality, it is the site we use to express it. Once the body ceases functioning, our spirit, no matter how young and fresh, leaves us. Today, unfortunately, we can, in our rush-about society, cease functioning as a body even before we die. Even dragging ourselves up the Stairmaster doesn't certify that we love, know, and relish our bodies, because health is not holiness, though it comes from that idea. Perhaps we can come back to some semblance of companionship with our bodies and their sacral qualities by caring for someone else's. Infancy and children introduce us again, with a bang, to this inherent notion; let's hang on to it this time.

WHAT PHYSICAL CARE ACCOMPLISHES

Seemingly unremarkable as it often is, physical care in family life is a series of miniature dependencies, little acts of give and take, hardly noted, which are like finely wrought strands collecting and weaving us together. As simple as holding open a coat, tying yet another shoelace, or pouring a plastic cup of milk, physical care of family members is the same all over. It's a work that never changes. Families everywhere must be fed, sheltered, warmed, and held. These are the universal tasks of caregivers. But in the end it is the way in which we do these everyday tasks, the spirit in which they are done, that determines the atmosphere of a family. It is the way we feed each other, bathe, groom, clothe, and lay us down at night that makes a family.

One of the most significant things we do as families is accompany each other through the stages our bodies manifest over a lifetime—not just when we are ill, or until our children are grown, or we ourselves are aged. Indeed, the latter is an impoverished perspective that causes us to miss the simple, most direct forms of intimacy and comfort. What our everyday physical life is together, as families, charts a story as surely as the photo album. Caring for each other's bodies, and claiming all the joy that act delivers, brings new vitality to our relationships. Just as we use our bodies to play in the most abandoned, authentic way, we need to be bodily present to receive the full benefits of family life. Yet, caring for the body of another does not come easily to most of us modern creatures. Current child-care manuals move from a complete focus on the physical care of infants to the psychological development of toddlers and rarely return to the subject of body again.

Daily physical care past infancy is unheralded in family life; we tend to do it as a kind of unspoken maintenance fee, instead of as the investment it is. In times of illness, we rush to get everybody better and back on their feet, without seeing the benefit that awaits us in a sickroom. It can be a time of vulnerability and *dependency* to reconfirm why we are families. *Dependency.* The word has an ugly ring to most of us. We have been trained to stand on our own two feet from the time we were knee high. Yet, the truth is that we are dependent on one another, and the body.

Lev Tolstoy, in *Anna Karenina,* paints a magnificent scene of the power of physical care when Constantine Levin lays eyes on his brother Nicholas, whose decrepit body has been dissipated by loose women, gambling, and crime. Constantine cannot look upon his brother, who lies dying in a cheap boardinghouse, without falling into an agitated state. "He smelled the frightful stench, saw the filth and disorder, his [brother's] agonizing posture, heard his groans, and felt it was impossible to help. It never even entered his mind to think of analyzing all the details of the sick man's condition, to think of how this body of his was lying there, under the blanket, how those emaciated legs, loins, and spine were doubled up, or whether it was possible somehow to arrange them better. . . . A cold shiver ran along his spine at the mere thought of all these details."

Constantine's wife, Kitty, who insists on accompanying him to the boardinghouse, reacts quite differently. Her pity, Tolstoy writes, "did not produce anything like the feeling of horror and loathing it did in Levin, but the need to act, to learn all about the details of his condition and to help him." Kitty sets about giving orders to her husband, her servant, as well as the prostitute who lives with Nicholas. They clean, sweep, and go for a doctor. A meal is served, the sheets are changed, and Nicholas's nightshirt is peeled off his "long white skeleton" of a body. At the end of this scene, Tolstoy continues, "The invalid himself, combed and washed, was lying on clean sheets, his pillows piled high up, in a clean nightshirt with a white collar round his unnaturally thin neck, staring fixedly at Kitty with a new expression of hope."

The effects of Kitty's work stretch far beyond giving a dying man physical comfort and a burst of hope and felt dignity. But it is not just the presence of illness which can plunge us into a more profound experience with each other's bodies; we can bring this hope to one another without the onslaught of serious illness. Caring for the body is a day-to-day task. It is a simple squeeze of the shoulder in passing. It is an offer to draw a hot bath. It is the purchase of a necklace or chain to adorn a body.

Yet the question remains. Why is it so hard for Constantine to care for his dying brother? Why is it so hard to touch? And even more strangely, why can it be so hard to touch members of our own family?

TOUCH

Every day, as we move through the world, our bodies are touched. We brush against strangers at the supermarket, our shoulders are burdened by heavy bags, and we suffer the undignified swats of turnstiles. Even gravity is a kind of touch. Yet, all these forms of touch are impersonal. They do not heal. There is a world of difference when we are stroked by a person who chooses to do so. That type of touch refreshes us. It sinks through to our spirits, our psyches.

Ultimately, touch is personal; it is intimate. It makes us vulnerable, both to touch and to be touched. Touch is a language that exposes us as much as the words we speak. It claims us and we claim others, as ours, with it. It's always telling, touch is, it reveals where you stand with another, unmitigated by words. Touch is instant, touch is immediate. Touch is the most distilled form of expressing care. Benedictions come out of it.

Back to Tolstoy. He does not let Constantine off the hook. Nicholas makes a last request—that he be turned over on his left side so he can go to sleep. Kitty is not strong enough to move her brother-in-law to his favored side. The act falls to Constantine, who, thrusting his arms under the blanket to gain a firm hold, is struck by the heaviness of his brother's emaciated limbs. The task completed, Nicholas holds his brother's hand in his own, and Constantine surrenders "with a sinking heart. Yes—Nicholas pulled it to his mouth and kissed it. Constantine started shaking with sobs; unable to say a word, he went out of the room."

One can perhaps forgive Constantine for not wanting to touch a brother whose body was in a decrepit state, or face the intimacy the act inscribes. Most of us can't use that excuse. It is ironic in an era like ours, so consumed with the body and its appearance, that we are so incompetent when it comes to the art of touch. We spend billions of dollars on cosmetics, gym membership, plastic surgery, and yet so many of us, women and men, detest the way we look, fear being touched. What is it about touch that makes us so uncomfortable? And how can we regain touch in our families?

CULTURES OF TOUCH

It is important to understand the era in which we live, because culture plays a central role in the experience of touch. This is especially evident in how people of differing cultures handle newborns. Kenyans actually toss them in the air to get them used to life on earth, while the American Indian traditions proceed in the exact opposite way—their children are swaddled to keep them from being startled.

In our public American culture, which effects our at-home traditions, touch has been captured for its market value. Our society is so sexualized, it hampers us from caring for our bodies—our own and each other's. This paltry spirit has even trickled down to affect relations with our children. And it has frozen us, frozen our touch. Contrary to the myths of our age, we are not really more physically free—quite the opposite, we now are obsessed with abuse, fear of deformity, age, illness, and death.

A *New York Times* article revealed that high school students, after physical education classes, no longer shower, as students of their parents' generation did. This is due, the article said, to students being bombarded with sexual imagery. American youth are so aware of what the "perfect" body looks like, that they—many of whom might qualify as the culture's ideal specimens—do not want to show themselves in a school shower.

This timidity is not only the province of the locker room. In this age, suspicion is attached to many forms of touch. Teachers and camp counselors cannot touch children for fear of being accused of molestation. Co-workers cannot touch each other for fear of being accused of harassment. We are conditioned by the cultural atmosphere to read every touch and understand every relationship for its lurking sexual content. While we all should be wary of these abuses of touch, we know that something profound has been lost in this cultural milieu. Sexualism has claimed everyday sensuality.

As families, we have to wrest back sensuality from the fashion photographers and alcohol advertisers by recognizing each other's bodies as the true miracles of flesh they are, not objects suited up for sale. Families have the power to mitigate the sexualized atmosphere around us. We set the tone of touch in our own little orbits of everydayness. Care for someone else's body gives it value beyond its current capitalization. When a husband yells from the bathroom, "Hey, want your hair washed tonight?" it isn't only hair that gets salon treatment, so does the whole self.

What is needed is to claim a sensualist point of view. However, everyday sensuality is only possible if we view the body as sacred and whole, having many needs: life, change, rest, and beauty—not just complaisant pleasure. To be sensual is to live within the sacred, not functional, needs of our bodies. To be sensual is to be receptive to what is truly good for our bodies in all their highly idiosyncratic dispositions, not to indulgences that dissipate the flesh.

Sensuality, which feeds our bodies and souls from the same plate, is the antidote to consumer sexualization. We are born sensualists, all of us, mothers, fathers, children. Sensing, sensate beings who must be touched, fed, blessed by water, warmth, and light. Old and young, we never escape these needs. Who would want to?

We can be sure that touch is never neutral. Like everything sacred its misuse is just as powerful in its effects as its use for healing. Eruptions of violence, especially at their most intimate, are also connected with the touch—the same longing to reconcile also fuels violence. We can't in this age discuss family touch without immediately thinking of abuse, but fear of this mustn't deny us a physical life as families.

Families are complicated weavings of light and dark, of hurt and healing. We will hurt each other in ways we didn't intend. We will even hurt each other intentionally. We will touch each other in ways we didn't mean—bursts of grabbing, snapping when irritations peak, followed either by remorse or escalation. But our hands can heal, no matter how rudimentarily applied. This healing power comes as part of our bodies. It cannot be lost—only, for a time, like anything sacred, be hidden from view. Our hands will always have the touch.

FACE AND HANDS AS SITES OF SENSUALITY

Saul Bellow in *Herzog* describes the problem of being alone inside one's body. Encased as we are, touch is one of the few physical, immediate gestures we have to bridge that aloneness, that philosophical, spiritual loneliness, and there are some specific sites along the body that are especially receptive.

The highest artistic figures, Michelangelo and Rembrandt, considered a work of human art incomplete without the presence of the face and hands. They were only echoing what cave paintings also tell. Apart from the magical, almost impersonal, powers of blood and penis, the parts of the body that most express and contain ourselves are our face and hands. It is the face and hands that are left unclothed and remain the most available, receptive, and sensitive to touch. Touching these constitutes a specialized sign of affection and grace. While all of the body is precious, the face and hands, the world over, are especially treasured. Hands are the instruments of love, holding hands is a universally performed act of affiliation. The touch of a hand contains as much language as a kind word. We can use this language to enhance our everyday life, to strengthen ourselves and each other. And to touch, to kiss a face is a beautiful symbol, a gesture of accepting the identity behind it.

THE BODY DEPENDENT

Sexualization is not the only force today that obstructs care of the body. Self-sufficiency and the values of independence improperly weighted against a life together also stymie us. We're leery of leaning unnecessarily on others, but that attitude leaves little room for a meaningful family life. Dependencies within a family—the thing our culture hints we must not only avoid, but even repent of—are the very things that help us find rest, aid, and comfort. Without true dependency, rest and relief are impossible, because we are not really the best persons to take care of our bodies. Oh, sure, you can do the maintenance stuff, but dwell on the elevation and sense of worth you feel when someone massages your hand or changes the dressing on a wound. Most often this care comes from within the family, because the home is where we haul our beaten bodies every evening, and it's the people at home to whom we entrust our growling stomachs, sore necks, and itchy backs.

A rubdown from a professional does wonders for our muscles, but it cannot compare with a massage given by a willing partner who by touch is treating more than aches. A back rub from someone who knows you and shares your life is a tacit confession that it's a tough world and you're in it together; just the sort of message that you want to hear at home. Home is a sought and welcome place after leaving the kind of work where we stare into a computer screen all day as if it were Narcissus' pool.

Dependencies also overturn a solely mechanical view of the body—that the body is natural and only natural and can be

well managed with good nutrition, proper exercise, and sup-
plemental vitamins. If you manage to drink eight glasses of
water a day, you're a genius at body management. But that is
not all the body is or requires. Someone else's care of your
body implies a relationship and as we well know, relationships
are never mechanical. Taking care of each other may be as
simple as bringing a cup of tea on a fancy tray to someone in
the bathtub. It is acknowledging that we each are bodies that
need care.

Tom is a traveling consultant and his wife is a nurse. He
recounts what comes to mind when asked about caring for his
wife. "When she's had a late shift, she is weary and I just
don't want her to be faced with a pile of dishes when she
comes home. Often I do the dishes—not because I want a
clean sink, though I do, or I feel compelled to do them because it is a part of my responsibilities and I'm often away,
but simply because I don't want her to do yet another pile of
dishes. I actually hate doing the dishes. The only time I really
enjoy it is when I make myself do them so that she won't have
to. You know, I don't even think she knows it, but I do."

Chris is another body-caring husband. He arranges dinners
for his wife. Not just carry-in, mind you, but dinner parties.
He calls me up and says, "Wendy has just finished a very
tough semester and I want her to relax. She does that best
with her women friends, so I'm making dinner for about six
of you. Will you come? No, don't bring anything, I'll do it
all, just come and have dinner with her." When you arrive, he
stands at the door, aproned, with intense smells wafting from
the kitchen, and directs you to a table he has set with candles,
flowers, cheeses, and olives and bids you to sit. Wendy arrives
and is astonished as she walks into the apartment and is im-

mediately handed a glass of wine, pecked on the cheek, pushed into the dining room, and ordered, "Relax." That's it. For the rest of the evening, a long and laugh-filled, sigh-filled one, Chris only appears to serve various courses, the last being a tray of chilled chocolates.

Family physical care, of course, transcends not only husband and wifely care, but even generations. The moment I cross my mother's threshold with my children, she arranges a time to brush our hair. They're private sittings and not just functional, mind you, but long sessions, surely a hundred strokes, accompanied by lots of chatting and subtle inquires about how our lives are going and could anything be troubling us.

ALLOWING YOUR CHILDREN TO CARE FOR YOU

We can give our children new identities by asking them to care for us. One evening, when my children were hardly older than tots, they recognized that I was so exhausted that they put me to bed, complete with a tuck, a song, kisses, and a softly switched-off light. To this day, I don't know how they got to bed themselves, but I do know without doubt that they found great pleasure in taking care of me, and in that moment they changed. Small as they were they had something to give and a place to give it. Seems there's no point in lavishing your family's bodies if you are not lavished back, and not just that sweet, usually inedible, breakfast on Mother's Day.

Teaching your children how to care for you is a deeper, healthier way to be a family. Having one's own physical needs respected, recognized, and met can also, surprisingly, build a common identity. In it we teach our children how to be a present and needed part of our own family and also to be future partners in the families they make—especially little girls, who are subtly taught at a young age to be attentive to the needs of others, but not how to ask for what they want themselves. Giving little boys practice helps them grow up comfortable with giving bodily care. A mother, a father, who asks for and expects help, aid, and care from their children is not burdening them with too much, but engaging them in the realities of human limitations. Expecting each other to be aware of different physical needs brings an added sense of responsibility, of humanity, for one another and a stronger family identity.

When I was large with child, my five-year-old became the Bend-Over Person. All things dropped fell into his domain. Though he expressed moments of exasperation—did you ever notice how much pregnant women drop things?—occasionally, at the door, as I was getting ready to go out, a sweet voice from an unseen boy would drift up, "Mommy, let me tie your shoes." I walked publicly and proudly with laces done in tortured knots, deeply thankful my shoes were not tied to each other. Yes, I bought him candy when we got to the store. Had he but known, he could have had anything he wanted.

WHEN CHILDREN CARE FOR EACH OTHER

Most children the world over take care of each other. Siblings, cousins, neighbors, are caretakers at a much earlier age than we allow in our culture, though images of little rascals, the small ones hauling the smaller ones heavily around to various escapades, may come to mind. In this we have lost something, not gained. Though interest in babies is displayed more often by girls, they are often primed to show interest and there is no reason why boys cannot be also primed. Young boys in most other cultures are involved in child care, carrying, feeding, playing, until they are segregated to work with the men. There's a lesson here for us. We allow children to be playmates, but somehow we think it is inappropriate to let children take care of each other, as if we are shirking our responsibilities as adults. That's supposed to be our job. But it's a great gift to give our children—to teach and prepare them to be interested in taking care of each other—not only for help in our daily lives, but for their adult lives later together. A few small baby bumps are but little cost, even to the baby, for promoting a family which knows how to pat and comfort one another in just that family way.

Families transmit their language of touch, their style of care, as much as they do inflections of voice and gesture. I watched my little children touching our newborn, as we gave them each getting-to-know-you time, alone with the baby in their own beds. Their hands traced out the exact pattern of stroking—across the cup of the head—as they had seen me do, indeed, as they had felt on their own little bald cups when they were of comparable size.

Children of other cultures who are consistently companions to each other, including physical care of each other, go on to deeper relationships of respect and reciprocity throughout their lives. Cross-cultural studies show that children of the same household who are provided with time to be together and take care of each other also segregate later and less often into both same-age and same-sex groups when they move out into the larger community of children. They feel comfortable being with children of a variety of ages, both boys and girls. Sibling rivalry does not have to be a dominant theme in sibling relationships, especially if we, as parents, lubricate the jealous moments we all experience with plenty of pats, squeezes, snuzzles, and "Would you like some jam and bread on your own little tea tray?" for the offended party.

Stepfamilies especially benefit when new siblings are expected to care for one another in practical ways. When they are given opportunities to care for one another, even as they are getting to know each other, and to be taken care of themselves, it stabilizes them again after loss and gives them somewhere again to belong, to give their efforts. It reassures them that they, too, will be taken care of and that a family is made up of people who take care of each other, each day. One smart, newly synthesized family with kids from both previous families had the children, seventeen, twelve, ten, and eight, cook for each other on a weekly, rotating basis. Groans came when it was the youngest's turn, but eventually they worked out a system to assist her. That was the night they had cheese sandwiches and malts. As siblings in later life they might have to deal with high cholesterol levels, but it seems a manageable price to build a family.

SPOUSES

"With my body, I thee worship." This line comes not from a hedonistic sex manual, but from marriage liturgy in the Anglican Book of Common Prayer. Its meaning is quite clear: that bodies are a medium—like incense or tapers—in an act of adoration—in this case, for one's spouse. Throughout the world, religious worship is performed with various elements—robes, song, food (mundane and celestial), bells, and dance—in short, things that affect our senses. It is through our senses that we come into touch with God and love, et cetera. In marriage, the vehicle of worship—the sensory path that brings us to deeper love—is care for one another's bodies. This call is issued not only to women, but also to men, in marriage. It might be a great conversation, next time you're out to dinner alone, to ask your husband what his plans are for worshiping you. Do you hesitate? Why? For women, it can be that they've grown up in cultural environments where they are likely to give without asking for reciprocity. Add to that the ridiculous cultural expectation that a "great lover" knows just what you want and when you need it, and you find women who have gone eighteen months without getting their hair washed and combed by their spouses, who are probably more than willing to do so if asked. Yes, it is important to ask. And it becomes easier with the fundamental belief that you cannot live without touch, just as you cannot live without food. Babies who are stroked, held, and rocked thrive; those who miss that, struggle. Why should touch become any less important in adulthood? Why does it disappear—except for sex—when couples walk down the aisle in marriage? The wedding liturgy also says, "To have and to hold." So, when you ask your spouse for a foot rub, you are asking to be held—asking him for a kind of spiritual food that you cannot live without. That touch will not only perform the mundane but necessary task of easing stress and loosening muscles, but make you stronger allies in the harsh world, and, surprise, keep your marriage sacred. There are two routes of remedy leading to a happier family life. Each route has to be traveled by both spouses, and eventually children will come onto this path. The first is to ask, "What would you like, what do you need?" The second is to ask for what *you* like and what *you* need. Touch will always be on the route.

A LIFETIME OF BODILY CARE

We don't just raise our children into healthy young adults and wave good-bye. Our children, our families, come to us for life, and that's what we want in the end anyway. We do live out our lives together physically, with seasons of hands-on, hands-off. And we ourselves will age as our children mature. We, too, will have changing physical needs, stages when we want to be closer, and stages when we like some space and independence. Each new stage requires recrafting our physical presence with each other. Touch and care in general, change over the life span; babies, teenagers, newlyweds, older couples, all need different manifestations. That dynamic keeps things interesting.

We have to make a family that heals its members, even when they are not physically present, by astute use of our love, our touch, and the comforts we cast out to each other that are carried into a lifetime. When we make our families, as we are growing them, all these little acts accumulate in their power. What counts about families is that they are there to come back to. It may be only memories of your mother's well-timed cup of tea, comforting you as you order up from a surly waiter in an anonymous café, but your family travels with you.

SPECIALIZED BODIES

As we move through bodily stages together, there are some special stages that are worth thinking of in advance. Pregnancy is one, of course, and babies. Nothing is more inescapably BODY than birth—for the mother, both through her pregnancy and the labor and delivery of the baby. In birth, the body gets to drive the soul for a change and one's soul is on for the wild ride, whatever happens. What does the woman deliver, after all, but a body, this little lamblike creature packaged in a now wholly-other body? What does she deliver but a body—and what do she and Daddy count but a body's toes, a body's fingers? In these small ways we acknowledge our wholeness, our physical sacredness.

MEN AND PREGNANCY

Yes, birth is the body, and for women it is manifestly given. But one should note that the world over, there is a complementary effort by men to try to counterbalance the impressive power of women who have the potential of birth, whether it is actualized or not. Men, too, have moments of making special use of their bodies. Men make quests, and perform feats of extraordinary effort, to put their bodies on the line in some attempt to match birth. There is a widespread practice, in Latin America, Asia, and India called "couvade"—in essence, men psychosomatically experience the traits of their wives' pregnancies. It is a great honor for men to be smitten with such an experience. They revel and boast of their morning sickness and backaches. They practice food aversions, restrict their usual activities, and parade an unnaturally enlarged abdomen in the village square. Some even go into seclusion after delivery, and emerge triumphantly claiming paternity. Compared to this, it seems a little mild to send our men out for pickles and ice cream.

For modern men, pregnancy means two things, not one integral, unfolding experience, as for women. First, they must cope with a partner undergoing tremendous physical change. In essence, they are no longer dealing with the same body. It's a stressful experience, and many men fear they will never see their old partner again, quite literally. They listen to their wives agonize about weight gain and swollen ankles, and secretly grieve the loss, all the while maintaining a show of faith, for their wives, for themselves, that it will come to a happy ending. And on top of that, they must then forge a new relationship with the party responsible for this, someone they can neither see, nor touch, indeed, can hardly believe exists! Women at least get touched by their in-utero babies, even if it's a swift kick from the inside.

"Hey, it's Daddy," my husband said rather sheepishly into my belly one night. This seemed to me quite amusing, as if the baby needed an introduction to one half of his own genetic material. Then suddenly it struck me that I had never considered introducing myself to the baby, announcerlike over an intercom—"This is your mother speaking"—because I felt the bodily connection so inexorably. I knew I was well known to the baby, but my husband had no such advantage. He had to make connections in other physical ways, in this case using his voice.

Making a family where men touch, speak, and care for

children is a vital way to connect them to their own progeny; many cultures, including our own, can often deny men this connection. Perhaps you have been stopped in your tracks, as I have, over the recent spate of advertisements of bare-chested men holding tiny babies. Do advertisers, more than Freud, know what women want? Yes! We want to see our handsome men holding babies, snoozing with them, schmoozing with them in chest-to-chest communion. As Jane Austen asks, "What attaches us to life?" Anyone who lays on hands gets attached to life.

BROKEN BODIES

We are never more crushed than when there is trouble at birth. No sadness holds for us the power of an incomplete body, a broken body. We grieve and turn heart stricken at this time like no other. In moments like these we can only comfort ourselves, with love, that love would allow us to care for this child when many would not be able to do so. We hope to find ourselves the kind of people who could, in such circumstances, make a life for a whole person, with an incomplete body.

When our neighbor's son was born with a leaking heart, an old-fashioned "blue baby," and destined to die without surgical repair, they learned quickly that all they could give him, all he could receive as a newborn, was the small, inconsequential daily care of the body, gentle changing, warm nursings, their breath upon his face. Perhaps, they said, it would be all he would ever get. In that season of attention, we watched and learned the significance of loving a body. A body, how-

ever small, records every trace of touch; it is never unconscious; unlike the mind, a body is never without sensing, even
in sleep. A body will always remember.

BABIES' BODIES, CHILDREN'S BODIES

Like play, looking at the body of an infant returns us to
childhood. Babies' bodies are a special form of being human,
and they elicit in us essential, elemental emotions. They infect
us with longing for the integration, the wholeness, they have.
As new parents, we experience again all the helpless and exu-
berant feelings of children, the unfeigned marvelling over everything manifested by a baby, a physical miracle. We cannot
contain our awe, expressing it to everyone within earshot.
New parents on the street can always be identified by their
aura of vulnerability; they've shed the social cloth that keeps
us all appropriately attired to go about our work. Instead, just
like the baby, they are naked to everything good. They blink
and look around, bemused, tired, and delighted. You will
notice they always smile at you at the crosswalk—it is a secret,
initiated smile. They assume you either know what they are
smiling about or wish that you did. What is it they know?
Their babies made them once again aware of the pleasures of
physical delight.

To care for an infant is a test of our humanness, a trial by
fire and love. What is good about caring for infants is that
they never let us forget how essential the body is. They snuf-
fle, bawl, and demand attendance. "Feed me, change me,
hold me," for an eternity of right-nows. And when they sleep,
it's as if they have cast themselves on a thin but safe shelf of

floating wholeness, complete integration. They show us what we once were, without guile, delightedly in love with our own body.

When infants turn into toddlers, the body is still in front, still demanding, but in a bigger world. Now protection from bodily harm becomes a concern of everyday physical life together. We aren't as impressed by the bodily transmogrification that takes place in front of us, because we've learned to live with it happening every day, day to day. It's impossible for the same miracle to impress us the same way over and over again. Thus begins the very fading away of the lesson we most need from our children—that there is intense pleasure in the active human body.

Right under our noses they play. They play and play and we watch and nod as if this itself isn't a further miracle. What do infants do when they get control of themselves, but move, explore, experience exhilarated delight in their bodies and what they can do. Their essence is to enjoy themselves as bodies, all over. It is through our children that we have a chance again to return to childhood ourselves, with all our attendant experience as adults, sobered but joyful. Through physical life with our children, through care of them and play with them, the hands-on of it, we again acquire our innocent selves, a delight in each other and the world around us. We discover all over again the potentialities of the senses. This is the heart of being with young children. As our children age we must struggle to keep this alive for ourselves, for them, in one form or another, as the world begins its intrusion into our family lives. This may be as simple as pointing out that a flower is beautiful, that rain smells divine, that a hand held feels warm and comfortingly sweet, that nothing satisfies like cool water reminding them we are bodies together.

Once children hit the walking stage and beyond, we spend more time explaining compared with the time we spent holding. Yet there are still many miniature ways of communicating with one's body. It's active use—a nod, a wink, a hug—are all fleeting acts of committing one's body, however momentarily, to another. Looks, touches, squeezes, physical smiles, a physical vocabulary—aren't they what children long for? Indeed, isn't that exactly what we thrill to in a romance—those little signals that you belong to each other—and isn't that what we end up complaining of missing when our marriages seem stale? It isn't just for romance that these things work, though it is there that we most seem to notice them. All of family life can capitalize on a richer life with each other's bodies.

SLEEPING BODIES

How we send our children off to sleep is also a deeply traced moment, recalled whenever we lay our bodies down; it's a shaky passing from one kind of reality to another. The atmosphere we remember will envelop us all over again, whether in cradles, that first dorm bed, or a hotel room. Family sleeping arrangements are as varied as forms of touch. In Tawai villages in Eastern Africa, a father must never enter the house a mother and child sleep in: he has his own sleeping lodge. Taira fathers (from Okinawa) take over sleeping with young children that mothers are attempting to wean. In many Latin cultures, it is siblings who sleep together, not mothers and children. In cultures where parents must get up and go to work in the morning, most babies sleep nearby in baskets, bassinets, or cribs. Whatever the arrangements, whatever the place, the tenderness we give to young sleepers will put their bodies to rest, not just for the night, but for a lifetime of nights.

Sheryl, mother of four, puts her children to bed with an orthodox blessing from the Book of Isaiah each night. Standing at the edge of their beds, hand on head, she uses each one's name, so they know it's meant strictly for them. "May the Lord keep you and bless you, dear child, and make His face shine upon you."

TEEN BODIES

Just when we've got the touching down, our children turn into abstainers. This is a cultural phenomenon, not a physiological one. It is not so in other places, other times. Lots of people have tried to answer for the adolescent crisis, notably Margaret Mead. From her fieldwork in Samoa she showed that not every culture has adolescents who go through the, shall we say, tumultuous years, who reject every hug outright. But, alas, our lot is cast with a culture that promotes distinct teen identity, complete with separate phones. Samoans we're not. What we can know from this is that it is not violating nature to touch a teenager, even their hair. We should really try to be creative in caring for a teen body, as they are special bodies, too, as special as infants'. Infant bodies and teen bodies are transitional bodies. They won't be around very long before they settle into a different form, but during the passage, it's the proverbial bumpy ride. As in all crossings, special preparation is needed for safe arrival on the other side. The care we give our teenagers will most likely approximate how we care for them as adults; and we will spend most of our life with our children as adults in adult bodies. This is a daunting thought, one you might want to put away and not think about until your children are teens. Nonetheless, when they get there, it's especially important not to give up too easily or too much. We can continue to have the pleasure and satisfaction of caring for our family's bodies.

"Our boy went on his first solo trip, to Toronto," told a father describing life with his teenage son. "Of course, he doesn't let us hug or kiss him like we used to, but, wouldn't you know, about two days after he got home, he plopped his big, long, gangly body down on the couch next to me and propped his head upon my arm as I read the paper. I froze, just looking at that glossy head, and locked my arm so it wouldn't move, savoring that affection. It felt every bit as electrifying as when I first held him as a baby. Maybe even more, because it was my fifteen-year-old son."

Living with teen bodies is also about preparing them for sexual maturity. Of course, you've been doing that all along, but this is intensive training.

Tina tells me she plans a joyous event to relish and celebrate Ariella's arrival at puberty. "I've told her when she has her first period, she and I shall be equals in terms of being women who can procreate. We shall have a tête-à-tête and save up to take a trip, just she and I. She will receive my Russian grandmother's ring, passed down from daughter to daughter, though I think she will be the only one to get it for this occasion. All the others received it for their sixteenth coming out, but we are in a new age and I feel young teen-agers need new signals to confirm their place." I thought this a remarkable choice a mother was making to celebrate her daughter's body. "Then my son said that he, too, was looking forward to being a man and he'd like a ring, so now I have to come up with something to mark his passage, or passages, away from childhood!"

BODIES AWAY

Babette sends her son vitamins through the mail, but anonymously signs the card, *From an admirer.* "I know he'd never take them if I offered them at home," she remarked. "But I plan to tell him who his admirer is when he's old enough to handle it!" When asked when she thought that would be, she said, "Late thirties, we'll see."

Caring for bodies away from us is hard work because we cannot resort to simple acts of hugs, tucking someone away for the night, preparing a meal, covering them with an umbrella. A mailed package of cookies gone stale in transit can never do the same work, except perhaps if one has been, over a lifetime, active in expressive care and when the crumbling package arrives, it recalls a litany of those moments. Phone calls are obvious, because the voice remains powerful, no matter what, but something more subtle, like lighting a sabbath candle for your daughter away at college, at the same time she lights one in her lonely dorm room, may be a new idea to you. I know one family who does this. The real payoff with bodies away is the years of care you've applied, and how those accumulated moments have built up a bridge of physical love that can still keep you connected, even when parted.

OUR PARENTS' BODIES

When the author Mary Gordon, in *The New York Times Magazine* article "My Mother Is Speaking from the Desert," describes poignantly her life with her mother, wheelchair bound in a nursing home, she writes about having a body left to care for. In all the pains and struggle she describes, what is remarkable are the actions she takes to care for her mother's body. No matter how long we must care for our parent's body, no matter how painful it is, no matter how bitter or burdened we become, it seems we can find no rest until we lay their bodies to rest. There is a reason for this. Nothing is a more final confirmation of the life-giving sacredness of the body than death.

HONORING THE BODY ONE LAST TIME

One of the oldest funeral excavations on record found a Neanderthal male body, placed in the fetal position, and carpeted over with flowers. Newly uncovered grave sites in Eurasia, dating back some four thousand years, found a baby, no more than three months old, carefully wrapped in wool, with small flat stones covering its eyelids. Next to it was placed a baby bottle made from a sheep's udder and a precious little cup carved from horn. Honoring the body, right into death, is a distinctively human act, and families are first at both birth site and grave site. We adorn, anoint, and tattoo our bodies from time immemorial to mark them with reverence. And when we lose our bodies in death, we still treat them tenderly. So can we in life.

A SACRED CONCEPTION OF BODY

Caroline Bynum, one of my favorite historians, is a bird-tiny woman who has to stretch to speak over the podium to the large, eager audiences she always draws. I wondered, the first time I heard her lecture, if it was her own size, her own experience of herself as a body, that gave her such deep perception into her scholarship, respected worldwide, on the medieval concept of the body. She looks carefully at the texts and images of the day to illuminate how men and women of the medieval period conceptualized what it was to be a bodied self. While notions of the medieval body bring to mind flagellation, she offers a very different picture, one where the body is so profoundly sacred and central that the people of the period simply could not imagine occupying eternity without their bodies. When they went to heaven they were united with a renewed body, their old one restored, albeit with a few stigmatic marks to remind them of their personal history. That's how four historic centuries of men and women thought. I wonder now what medieval women and men would make of us, of the texts and images of our times, of our bodies? Would they be blessed in any way with the iconography we are surrounded with, from women's magazines, to film, to Times Square billboards? Would they have any sense at all that we consider our bodies sacred? A person of medieval times would be looking for signs of the body as a living gift from God and a beautiful gift that we give to one another. You may not be used to thinking of yourself as a natural icon of beauty, a symbol of living and embodied grace, even though it is easy and natural to think of your children that way, but if you don't recognize yourself as miraculous flesh, it's because our experience of ourselves as bodies has been profoundly interfered with by commercial ambition. Not to mention that as bodies today, we are chronically exhausted. It's a condition that comes with our era. In fact, a meditation on bodies today cannot conclude without observing this fact. Much of our physical life feels like it's lived underwater, as if we're loaded down with the tonnage of an entire swimming pool over us, and lacking the vitalizing source of oxygen. If we rest, it is only to go back into the struggle; in the end it makes us bitter. Some notion, however slight, however glimmering, of the sacredness of the body calls us, like medieval people, to think about our bodies in front of God, in front of each other, where cell phones, whizzing cars, microwaves, and all the other mechanical things that speed up our lives are silenced. It is flesh and blood, as the medievals knew, that has inestimable worth and sacred delicacy.

Five

Ritual in Family Life

*M*y first family ritual was an accident. When my daughter was a newborn, I was alone, bathing her, and we seemed to slip into another time. The water, her miniature body, the soap, were no longer part of the everyday, the usual rub-a-dub-dub. The elements of the bath seemed clear and essential. Everything came sharply into focus. We both became alert, sensing something different. Some kind of crack in the usual routine had opened up to larger things.

I grabbed her little nude shoulders and, my voice echoing off the tiles, declared, "You are my daughter."

Immediately, I felt silly, but I knew we had crossed a divide. I'd been initiated into my new role. I rolled her up in a towel and we went on with the day, but I had felt a brief respite from being an inexperienced, raw mother. Our new life together had been acknowledged, credited, vaguely blessed, if only by me.

I had just stumbled on the power of a ritual to bind a family together. Though rituals are among the fundamentals that anthologists study, and I was thoroughly familiar with them from a studied point of view, until this experience I had never connected what rituals could mean to me. Sure, I'd gone through the obligatory wedding, and with joy, but this was different, a private ritual, over in a second, instantaneous. I began to think about the possibilities. What transforms the everyday into little rituals?

Rituals point us forward, they close the past, urging us to advance, supplying us with confidence to accept new roles. In previous times, this would have been provided naturally from some institutional or social source, a church, a synagogue, an extended family, but now we have to produce it ourselves. A baby shower does not help us change into a parent, though it gives us all the material instruments, the stroller, the blankets, the booties. Modern life has let ritual fall away from us. We've lost our sense of its rooting, fostering power, we've been cleaned up in the mobile machine age, like chrome, and sterilized. No smoky rites of passage for us. Yet, if we don't have rituals in our lives to mark occasions, great and small, we are living an unnatural life, one not wholly in keeping with true human aspirations.

A ritual, as scholars define it, is a special act that links people through shared meaning. It can last a moment or it can be repeated throughout a lifetime. The importance of ritual has recently come again to the fore, through the work of psychologists, who are using it more and more to help patients cross over from old hurts, and by sociologists, who are exploring ritual's emergence into public life, and by anthropologists, who, as always, hold ritual as vital and who are studying it in new forms—for example, the ritual associated with a trip to Disneyland or of sending your first child off to camp. These disciplines are helping to reestablish ritual's central cultural role. Ancient carnival celebrations in the Dolomites of northern Italy, for example, have recently been reintroduced by elders who can still recall the festivals of the 1920s. These carnivals not only reanimate a regional identity, but, of all things, promote tourism, surely a new and novel use of ritual. In Malta, as reported by Jeremy Boissevain, a noted anthropologist, young men have boisterously revitalized celebrations of neighborhood patron saints as a sort of anti-gang initiative. Though new or reinvented, these still match a more public, accepted understanding of ritual. Revitalization of public ritual is among us, but the use of it in a more personal forum gives it special meaning to family. One has to craft one's own to make them of value to the family.

Rituals, as language, play, memory, meaningful touch, and spiritual longing, are all distinctly human. Each of these aspects of our common humanness stands open for us to individually pursue, to deepen and engage. In that pursuit, we become more human, which is to say alive with awareness, powerful in making the meaning of things. God has explicitly invited us to this pursuit.

Rituals most intimately affect families, giving them a common focus, bringing them together in a way everyday activities cannot. Demanding jobs and busy schedules have eroded traditions as basic as the family dinner, the symbol of a well-ordered life. Lifestyle today erodes not only such traditions, but our whole sense of timing, pacing, of the appropriate and connected moments to go about our lives. Nonetheless there are still daily moments that lend themselves naturally to domestic ritual: exits and entrances, bathing and bedtime. These rituals are closer to us than we think, for they ride alongside the routine in our lives, waiting to break through when we are ready. Nor do we have to wait for them to strike. We can create them.

How do we make our own rituals? How are they different from mere habit? To do this we have to know what makes a ritual. Rituals arrest time, giving us a momentary respite from rush and routine: no ritual is rushed through. They open new chapters of our life; they heal by closing or buoying us over old hurts. Rituals change things, move things forward: they seal us together. Some of classical anthropology's most brilliant minds have been fascinated with ritual. They've taken it as their "play" topic; their "let's think!" topic. And while they have written seriously, one cannot quite describe the joy and exuberance leaking through their stiff dissertations on ritual.

Monica Wilson, an early researcher on African rituals, captured it most succinctly when she wrote, "Rituals reveal values at their deepest level . . . express[ing] what moves people most. I see, in the study of rituals, the key to an understanding of the essential constitution of human societies." In this, she pointed directly to the reason ritual holds such magnetism for the Big Thinkers of anthropology. By 1909 Big Thinker Arnold van Gennup had discovered ritual's essentials, "which accompany every change of place, state, social position, and age." In his famous book *Rites du Passage,* Claude Lévi-Strauss never stopped writing about the symbols of ritual which to him were always metaphorical and embodied sophistication at its zenith.

Victor Turner, who gave his entire career to his fascination with ritual, noted that ritual made a special community out of those who participated, binding them into a fellowship. We can think of sanctuary choirs to get a picture of what he meant. Once robed, the individuals are a unit.

While I am not trying to detach ritual from its community or religious moorings, family use of ritual takes place on a bit of a differing plane. I am quite convinced that we can invite ritual into our homes. We can become our own healers through the use of ritual; indeed we have to, since so much stabilizing social ritual has disappeared, leaving us adrift in our roles, our responsibilities, our gifts, our position toward each other, even in our families—most especially in our families. I think we can make our own kind of "domestic" rituals to salve us, bind us, give us rest.

There is a standard vocabulary to rituals—anointing oils, candles, dainty edibles, changes of costumes (think pajamas), water, incense, fire or smoke, wines and settling or unsettling drinks, a feather here or there, fresh fruits and flowers, darkness contrasting with light, slow time, music, the voice intoning a reading or song. They needn't all be present for a ritual to be the real thing, and this list is hardly exhaustive—you must only walk into a room with these things stocked on the mental shelf and ask, "What can I do with that?" A single candle can be so powerful. Ritual is a form of adult play, as sophisticated as Lévi-Strauss claimed, with flights of imagination quite beyond the routine of cassava production, but with serious purpose—to mark passage, to engender change, to heal, to transform. It can be that for us, too, as we get out our common, everyday objects and take a new look at them and their possible use in our life with each other.

Immutable, age-old ritual has more social power than invented ritual precisely because it cannot be innovated.

Nevertheless, invented rituals share some of the same potent properties. Our own rituals identify us as a family to each other and to the outward world.

When our children started school, my husband and I devised a morning exit rite. The last stop at the door, usually reserved for collar pulls and hair straightening, was transformed when I simply pressed my hand on their heads. "I'm sending you out to the world. Go on, but come back safe." My children would return to the door for that benediction if I'd forgotten it. They feel a difference between home and the world. Years ago I caught my three-year-old saying good-bye to his older sister. He reached up and put his hand on her brow, leaving behind a peanut butter smear. "Yuck!" she yelled, but she exited knowing she'd been marked to meet the world, and she would return from her adventures to a haven. Anointing one another doesn't have to be as formal as it sounds.

My writer husband, who works at home, struggles with the monotonies of caring for children. He, too, was looking for something to snap the hold of routine. Laundry is not considered a ritual at our house, but storytelling is. There are no books involved at bedtime. For years, my husband has been wildly dramatizing his own childhood history, playing dozens of roles, from elementary school teachers to a neighborhood librarian. The stories, which bridge imagination and memory, have accumulated into a giddy family saga, with wide-eyed children in attendance. They are at episode two thousand and I still have to come in and shut the lights.

In fact, our front door has become a ritual site. When we hung out a 1929 passport photo of my husband's grandfather right after his death, it attracted our neighbors' attention.

And there we stood, under the portal, exchanging stories of our immigrant grandparents' lives. After a few minutes, one neighbor ran back to her place and got a picture of her grandmother and mother, stiffly standing photo-studio style, concentrated expressions on their faces, two generations about to enter the New World. This picture launched a whole new chapter of immigration history, old-country recipes, and survived tough times. "I have a sense memory of exactly how my mother's hand felt on my hair," this neighbor said. We stood there, nodding, before we went in and softly closed all our doors. Rituals like these recall and revitalize memories.

Rituals can heal. As Vic Turner noted, "very often the decision to perform rituals was connected with crises," and in a high scholarly tone, he adds, "a multiplicity of conflict situations is correlated with a high frequency of ritual performance." Yes, I can second that. Ritual often serves to ease us over rough waters. I've come to think of rituals as a kind of homemade remedy applied to family scrapes and wounds. Friends of ours found a momentary relief from persistent bickering with a ten-year-old son when they started reading aloud to each other from favorite books. They set aside time, not long, on Friday evening, to read one chapter only, stay tuned for the next. The son now excitedly presents readings from the adventures of Tintin, a series of Belgian comic books. He holds up the pictures for his parents to gaze at.

On a sadder note, a husband of fifty years, though he didn't have the marriage he longed for, never failed to put his wife's slippers by her bed, anticipating the next day. This little act was not just a habit, it kept him going. It kept him going forward even through the sense of disappointment, loss, and grief he felt, but alive to what he did have.

Ritual, in fact, has come to the vital aid of the therapeutic profession. Many families suffering from crises can be woven back together through a ritual putting away of old hurts and a symbolic wiping the slate clean. An attitude of new life always engenders new possibilities. Rituals are used for abused children, enabling them to experience a rebirth into a new set of circumstances. Rituals, too, can be immensely useful to new stepfamilies trying to define their roles, their rights and responsibilities, with new members. Some families even practice an adoption rite for their new children, modeled on the marriage service. "I commit to be your new dad." Sounds a little hokey, but when that preteen says, "I commit to be your new daughter," something powerful has just hatched. Though you needn't be as formal as that, you can at least have your own private rituals with new stepchildren, even if it's Friday pizza, hockey outings, or simply giving them a gift of welcome. Stepfamilies are in the delicate place of having to replace old rituals associated with another life. Don't leave this undone.

In this we oughtn't forget the power of the voice to heal, bless, read, recite, or sing, or the place of sabbath. Sabbath as a ritual has a long history and probably accounts, in the end, for civilization. It is certainly civilizing in the best possible sense. Rest, ritual rest, which no one dares disturb, was thought up by God and passed on only to humans. Reading the Sunday newspaper was not thought up by God, but He's willing to enter into it a little bit, from accounts I'm told, if you put your feet up and, as you read, count your blessings.

As a contemporary twist on Sabbath rest, we have high tea on Sunday evenings. It waxes and wanes in its elaborateness. Certain plates and platters come out just for this event. They are nothing more than thrift-shop finds, but once they hit the table they become heroic, met with expectation and excitement. We light candles, sing, and nibble on treats. In the days of our early marriage when, as my father-in-law likes to put it, "we didn't have a pot to put a chicken in," our treat was popcorn. It didn't matter that we ate like birds, we still soared. We've graduated to Swiss chocolate, and sweet pear sandwiches—an invention of my son—but come measles or tax time, we still relish our tea together. Disappointment reigns if we miss it.

Nevertheless, miss it we do, and that is another lesson. Rituals lose their power if clung to too rigidly, with roles too prescribed. They work best when used flexibly, creatively. We've abandoned certain rituals and added others as our children grew. We no longer recite the ancestral origins of our children's features—your nose is from Auntie Gretchen, your hair is just like Nonna's—but we'll never give up our secret names for each other.

Older parents, friends of ours whom we've looked to many times for wisdom, have a ritual that came into being when their children were all grown up and making lives of their own. They call up their children, a son and daughter, to get together to make liqueurs for winter consumption. They act as if this were the frontier and they were stocking up for a snowbound season. First they go shopping together, snuffling around, poking, and taking only the choicest plums, brilliant tangerines, freshest ginger. They confess there is usually a lot of arguing over ingredients; resolution comes when they agree to buy everything. Loaded with bags, they then stop off at the vodka store, lug home a couple of gallons, and get to work, but not before breaking out the last bottle from the previous year. They mix and sip, boil and mutter, roiling around in a hot kitchen together, then bottle it all up until it distills months later. The serious matters start then, when decanting begins. As each batch is filtered into decorative bottles, the family members name it according to what they deem to be its essence. The plum liqueur last year, with a touch of clove and maple syrup, was "Ella Fitzgerald," a smoky-tasting bergamot was "Chesterton," and a crisp, tart ginger was "Ice Capades." They are longing to concoct a "Chrome Sling" or "Carmen Miranda," having no clue, as yet, what they will taste like. Though they carefully write everything down, every measurement, they never follow the recipe again, and each liqueur is essentially lost at the last drop. This is a ritual.

Some rituals are used just once. The family that waited seven years for a larger apartment anointed their new one by going from room to room with burning incense, thanking God for each room and saying a prayer over the use of it. Each member expressed what they hoped for from that room. They spent a long time in the kitchen, anticipating what would come out of it now that they had an oven, and bedrooms, one for each of them. An old ritual may be just the thing you need once in your life.

A FAMILY CALENDAR

Ceremonies and celebrations at births, weddings, reunions, and funerals are "how we change yet remain constant from one stage of life to another," wrote the author Robert Fulghum in his book *From Beginning to End: Rituals for Our Lives.* But these are the big moments of ritual, and the smaller, more intimate ones also weave us together. After several years of high teas, rounds of birthday parties, holidays, and anniversaries, it became apparent to me that there was a cycle, a recurrence, in all of this, though a very personal one, specific to our family. I began to orient myself to daily life depending on where we were in our family cycle, the family calendar, like an annual liturgical year.

We have our own commemorations, which include, like everyone else, the first lost tooth, but a ritual calendar has its own special metering, because each year that you come back to your ritual, the children are a year older. You, of course, will stay eternally young.

A calendar notion allows you to think about what is coming up next that you want to commemorate, even in the smallest way. After parent-teacher conferences, if they're good reports, one family takes each child out for ice cream sundaes. They always sit on the swiveling stools at the counter. I didn't feel I should ask if they had a ritual for bad reports.

Another family's calendar is more seasonal. They incorporate the newest crop at the green market, inaugurating the advent of peonies in the spring, pomegranates in the fall, pumpkins, of course, in October, and you can guess November and December because we all do those. These weave in with the rest of their lives, the birthday cakes, the first date, all those specialized moments of family life that really should be attended to, forthrightly acknowledged.

One family's calendar involves decade rituals; when each of them hits a new decade, a big party ensues. When their daughter turned ten, they invited all her friends, young and old, who each brought a gift, and passing her around the room, each recited a memory they had of her as a younger child, then a wish for what she would become.

These kinds of rituals mimic classic initiation rites, which can come in the institutional form of first communions, bar and bat mitzvahs, sweet sixteen parties, or *quinceañeras* bashes for Latin girls. While these events will certainly be on the family calendar, it is the handcrafted, intimate rituals that really hold us together, like the family that makes multicolored, swirled candles with their children. They burn them only for certain holidays or days special to their family, so that each year the candle they made burns a little lower.

Essential to ritual is the process of remembering, known as "invocation." Invocative stories are often not only the content of ritual, but become a ritual in the obligatory telling. Not only do we find rituals, but they, too, find us. Storytelling is the archtype ritual.

A friend, Alison, immediately offered this story when I told her my interest in ritual, illustrating that, given a chance to, we all can recall rituals in our lives. "When I was six," she stated, "my Airedale dog climbed up on the countertop and ate my birthday cake while all the children were waiting in the other room. From then on, every one of my birthday parties was inaugurated with this story and how we solved it by rushing to the store for Timmy Cakes, individually packaged." I'd never heard of Timmy Cakes, but I knew just what they must look like. *Timmy Cakes* are liturgical words in her life.

Indeed, story after story tumbled out of Alison, she could hardly stop herself, following me around with a cup of coffee as she identified more and more events in her family's life as rituals on the family calendar. "In my husband's family," she further offered, "everything was honored through cooking and food. Every celebration involves food, his whole family are brilliant cooks. His sister always makes a cranberry sauce from berries and whole oranges. Every one had their celebrity dishes. Uncles did pancakes.

"I guess every family is different," she went on. "Mine did storytelling. My grandmother traveled a lot and she got some type of a souvenir for all of us, frequently something to wear, and all the cousins would set her up in a chair and put together a performance—a play, a story—for her."

My own husband has a knack for asking, "What were we doing this time last year?" This knack has spontaneously erupted into annual traditions, like celebrating the day we moved to New York, the day we moved to our latest apartment, our first kiss, our first hampster. Mind you, most of these are celebrated only by cracking open a beer, but they are remembered and toasted, even if in between dishes and bedtime.

CHILDREN MAKING RITUALS

After all this, if you can't think of any rituals, ask your children—they surely will. My son's was making a monthly cake. He started at age three, dragging a heavy chair over to the countertop, stepping up, and commanding whatever ingredients struck his fancy. The first contained two eggs— personally cracked—two cups coarse salt, whole apples (two), flour (only one pinch), and unshelled peanuts. Mix. Of course we had to bake it, he would have been crestfallen otherwise. And we had to bake it for the longest amount on the timer. We waited an hour for the ding. "Mommy, let's do this again!" If you hear that, you have a potential ritual on your hands. He's still making those cakes, and is a better baker now, but the point really was, after all, doing something side by side that he could count on, that transformed us both—he got taller and in charge, I got the supporting role for a change, and we didn't let ordinary time or rules order us around.

Though cake making is rather pedestrian, as rituals go, we have friends who help their children get candles at the first accumulation of snow, place them in cut-out milk containers, and march out in the dark woods behind their house to half-bury them in a glowing circle. They then sit out with hot cocoa and tell stories or sing—a fine introduction to the winter season.

At a birthday party, it was our children who thought up a family tradition for the guests. Guests, adults, and children were told to scatter to every room and take whatever they wanted, depositing it in a circle in front of the couch. Then all adults were obligated to construct an adventure, picking up an object and elaborating on the tale to find a place for it, putting it back down when they wanted to pass on the story to the next adult. The story ended when every object had been used.

Children are especially good at concocting rituals for families strung out by distances, traveling parents, far-flung grandparents and aunties, or college-age brothers. While they usually resort to phones and photographs, they can nevertheless remain inventive. A sister whose older brother started his freshman year away, regularly sends him a stick of gum in an envelope. A kindergartner decided to draw half a picture, sending it over the fax to Grandfather, who had to finish it and send it back. They are developing a portfolio for exhibition in his basement. Cookies will be served opening night.

There are rituals that seem more clearly to contain the sacred, like a benediction at the door, a prayer or blessing at bedtime, or holiday singing, that make other rituals—like making a cake, keeping a regular phone call—seem pedestrian; but maybe not, maybe all these small acts, domestic rituals, are not so small after all.

My daughter, at eight, and I still have a bath-time ritual. We play Saturday beauty salon. I chew gum loudly, and do her hair. As I lather up, I ask questions in a heavy accent. "So, daaarling, how's the school situation?" Sure enough, I get a deluge of confidences I would never receive in the role of Mom. I keep her tacit confessions confidential; we never mention them in our regular rounds.

Lately, when we've been playing salon, we've switched roles and she has insisted that she be the beautician. I play "the most beautiful voman in the vorld" in the best neglected-Hollywood-star voice I can muster. I act hopelessly self-absorbed and vain, and she has to cope with me. She does pretty well at hiding her exasperation, although one time she said, as she twisted my hair extra hard, "Oh, I do this for all my victims."

I hope we still share this ritual in some fashion when she is on her own. It would be a moment we forged together over a lifetime. Maybe someday, when she's washing my hair, she'll ask, "So, daarling, how's the retirement situation?" Even better, maybe she'll say to her daughter, "Hey, wanna play beauty salon?"

Six

Family and Home

A Concept of Home

Mircea Eliade, a famous French scholar, thought of home as the first spot on the globe, the first place from which we look out at our world. "Nothing can be done, nothing can begin, without this initial orientation," he wrote. He saw the home not only as a place where we first look out to the horizon, but also the first point of our reach upward toward the heavens. Home is "a pillar which upholds the universe." Without home, chaos results. We know this. Home is a pillar we can hang on to, home is a haven, a site of memory, a place where we can invite the sacred to show itself; home is a link, a bridge, an integration point to the public world. Home is a gift. It's portable, because home is not just a place, it's a concept. It's inside us.

When cancer struck an American theologian living and teaching in Switzerland, his family called their son, a painter working in Boston. They explained that they needed a rental house for a month because his father would be taking treatments at the Mayo Clinic in Minnesota. They asked him to go there and find a place and get it ready for their arrival in two weeks. The son obliged and began a search for a suitable rental. When shown a place, he would carefully survey each room, taking so much time the real estate agent was at first curious, then impatient. What was there to see in these impersonal, nondescript rooms? All they needed was a clean set of beds, a bath, and a location within walking distance of the clinic. The son finally settled on a place, seemingly no different from any other, then flew back to his studio and got to work right away. In a frenzy, he executed eight different paintings over the next two weeks. He then arranged to have them shipped immediately and hung according to his exact instructions. They were there waiting when his family arrived, and when the father walked into the anonymous house he found paintings by his son in every room.

A month later, ready to return to Switzerland, the father called to ask his son what should be done with these valuable paintings. "Leave them. They were painted for you, while you were in that specific house, just for that time," said the son.

I have been shaped by this incident, even hearing it as I did as an impressionable twenty-four-year-old with no home yet of my own. I was so struck that someone would make such an effort to decorate a place for just a month—for such temporary accommodations. Why didn't they just live with what was there? What did they expect the paintings to do? How could someone expend such energy on something seemingly superficial when facing the threat of cancer?

I learned not only how much the environment we live in affects us, but also how much we can make out of each moment, each circumstance. Through the urgency of the necessary, we succumb to a utilitarian view of the home, just as we do with the care of our bodies, or with play. We allow ourselves to inhabit functional spaces, thinking them sufficient for our needs. The paintings were a way to assail this perspective. Those paintings were an act of love, painted, yes, for temporary circumstances, but as an eternal expression of compassion. They were an act, too, of assertion, of claiming a space so as to resist even passing anonymity. Above all, they were a gift, in the way flowers are a gift. The son's gift made a home for his father, a momentary one perhaps, but just as healing as a permanent home. In fact, the homes we make, transient or handed down through generations, are always a gift.

HOME AND MEMORY

I now try to make places I have to go to, even hotel rooms, a momentary home—bringing little personal effects to claim a space and make it mine. I didn't know until later that by doing this, I was, along with the family facing cancer, practicing a fancy Russian language theory.

The famous Russian linguist Victor Vygotsky distilled a version of his thoughts about language into the notion that it is language that allows us to accumulate memory. Without something to call our experiences we would have no way to store them all. His most interesting discovery, however, is that our memory is stored not only inside our language and inside our heads, but outside of our selves as well, in the visual and tactile cues we receive from the things around us.

If we see a certain object, whiff a certain scent, it recalls to us the experience once again—we remember fully what the past felt like. But for that waft of the summer smell in the grass, the sight of a specific cup—our retention of our history would be limited. If you were to sit down with a grandmother whose home is filled with seemingly irrelevant bric-a-brac and ask her what each piece is, they would all come alive with stories and people, each holding an important place in her life.

Vygotsky's theories are especially borne out in the experience of the aged, particularly those people placed in nursing homes or a new environment. After this transition, they often become disoriented and finally fail, though bodily cared for. They are losing their memory, not because they are getting old, but because they have lost contact with the objects that held their memories, memories stored in the minute things that once surrounded them. Even the shape of drawer handles, the length of the hallway, knowing exactly how high to lift one's foot to clear a step, are memories that acclimate us to specific places. We literally *recollect* as we orbit through our familiar spaces, moving our bodies in familiar ways, seeing our familiar trinkets, our daily items. All these details of life are not only the outward space we inhabit, but the tactile containers, the recepticles we use to hold our experiences. Here's where it pays to be a materialist—not for the hoarding of possessions of status, but as vessels of memories.

My mother has an old sauce pot whose lid never quite fits. In one and only one position would that silly lid not tip and fall into boiling water. Home for a visit, I rummaged through the back of the cabinet, determined to toss it out and get her one that wouldn't scald her. As I sat on the floor, searching the very back of the shelves for that mischievous lid, my mother came in. "What are you doing?" she asked. I explained my purpose, and she calmly got down on her stiff knees and, balancing herself, pulled the lid forward and matched it with the pot on the floor. "Here," she said, and she pointed to an arrow drawn on the pot. "And here." She pointed to an arrow drawn on the lid. "Before your father died, he drew these on to show me where the lid fits. Don't ever throw this out." There it is. That's the salve of materials things. That place, that pot, where the two arrows meet, that's home.

CREATING A HOME

Home is the first place we spend our love. It is the site, the space, the enclosure, where we love each other and spin ourselves into a family—mother, daughter, father, son, and over all, lovers. It is the place we disburse our energy, expend our life, and exercise our imagination. It holds all our little memory objects and, with them, the people we love—the ones we are willing to spend our lives on. The ones we most want to show and tell to. It's never just four walls. Home can be thought of almost as a body to care for, a body that contains the spirit of the family. One can read the character of a family by the home they make. It is not the things they have, but the spirit of life that is manifest in their home, because home is the ultimate joint project families do together.

It is imperative that home be made by all family members. It is not a woman's private project, whereby she creates a space and everyone else just inhabits it. Home is a joint project—that means children must be fully engaged in "keeping" house in the same way the adults are. Most chores for children are assigned to build character—not really to attend the body of the home together. By giving children an explanation about why their contribution to the home is important and giving them an opportunity to contribute—a true sense of ownership—a discernible difference in the attitude takes place; it's a community effort. Young children "play house" for real because they understand that you depend on them; and if they feel how vital they are to you, to this project, they respond. After all that is what children inherently want, to belong to someone, in some place, and to give their little selves too.

On a summer vacation to my hometown, a tiny village in Michigan's Upper Peninsula, it dawned on me to give my children a stake in the land during a walk through a forest. I called them over to me and said, "This is my land. I was born here. I own it, like the Indians own it. It's under my care." Then, with a slightly dramatic wave of my arm, I claimed, "And now, I give this land to you." My children's eyes lit up with this new idea, and they scampered down the trail in front of me with new energy. I noticed they bent over and picked up the Pepsi cans dropped occasionally on the path. Their ownership took root immediately. While I can't say the ownership principle has inspired them to pick up their socks from our bathroom floor with the same vigor, I believe the idea grows. I recently found my kids playing "chores." There's hope.

On the sock problem, a family we know plays "Cinderella" with their young daughter at housecleaning time. The mother becomes the evil stepmother and demands that Cinderella pick up her room. She carries on a made-up dialogue with Cinderella's imaginary mean and prissy stepsisters complaining about Cinderella's sloppy housekeeping. The daughter stage-weeps dramatically and, little by little, picks up her room. With this approach, Mom gets to play a little "house" too. Unfortunately, the daughter usually wants to play ballgown dress-up right after the socks are in the drawer and the toys are on the shelf—generating a new mess. This mom is working on breaking up the drama into Act I, Act II, hoping for a little space of neatness at intermission.

There are lots of ways to take possession of a living space. We name our furniture. At first it was simply an easy way to tell the children where to get something, without endless description. "It's in Greta," we'd shout from the back room instead of "try the cabinet next to the refrigerator." Now some slow transformation has taken place, and we have a Greta living with us. It's rather hard to explain, but surprise if that cabinet doesn't just look like a Greta, sort of very upright and proper. You should see Butler. He's a cast-off from an old university library—a card catalog—the kind of chest with all the little drawers for title cards. When the children were very little we would stock each drawer with a different toy: a rubber ball, cards, a yo-yo, Slinkys, tiny dolls, minicars, spoons, and china cups. Small visiting children would be introduced. "This is Butler, his bottom drawers are the best." He is part of the family, practically a beloved uncle.

IMAGINING A HOME

A home is made out of bodily needs. We have to eat, we have to rest, we have to sleep. What can we do with that? How can we use those needs to build relationships? That's the ultimate human trick—to raise up our bodily needs into lasting bonds. Home is not just meeting those needs, but building relationships out of them through so many little gestures, placements, coffee cups, shared dainties, boiled potatoes, and checkbooks. Home is just like those blocks out of which you used to make kindergarten houses. Each element adds until you have an entire construction, and you step proudly and excitedly back.

We have not only relationships with the people in our homes, but with our home as well. Like a relationship which passes through seasons, so can your affiliation with your home. The best way to inspire a family's relationship to their home is using nature's seasonal changes. Yes, there's spring cleaning and the hanging of holiday decorations come December. But I'm also talking about a way to do these tasks that goes beyond the motions of pure efficacy. Looking at a home with a new perspective and taking care of the home together allows us to take up housekeeping as an act of care, rather than a taxing routine that robs us of time to be with our loved ones. We have friends who, when they pull up the rugs during the spring, have a good time beating and rolling them up before bidding them adieu until fall. Then they spend a half hour sliding around in their socks on the hardwood floors. Home, too, needs to be refreshed and renewed as a physical space. As we begin to understand the concept of home, and its importance in building our relationships and memories, we can transform our experience from mundane tasks to a higher calling. Only laundry is exempt from this effect. For some reason, laundry, conceptually, cannot be transformed into anything more than laundry. At least I haven't found a way to do it. Perhaps someone bolder will. I will say that I've made progress with ironing, however—but only a certain kind. It has to be white linen tablecloths.

White linen tablecloths connect me to my grandmother— the one I never knew. I've been told again and again how she always had a pristine tablecloth on her humble Sunday table. In fact, as the iron glides and polishes the cloth, I feel connected to all the women who once ironed a tablecloth for a family occasion. It's a time I crave, so peaceful; the hiss and sizzle of an iron smoothing a beautiful white cloth transports me into the pantheon of women who sweated and cared to make a place a home. I love their fictive company.

We guard our things, too, as if they are relationships— which, in a way, they are. This involves moving things around, giving them a fresh place to be seen, packing them away, and bringing them out again to surprise us, so that familiarity doesn't breed blindness to their virtues.

The consumer world allows us to purchase our dwelling's history à la Ralph Lauren. We can buy new gingham sheets that look like they belonged to our grandmother, or we can go the Martha Stewart route and salvage antique linens from a tag sale. However, none of these purchases means anything until we place our own stamp on them, and we can only do this by loving them, relishing them, taking pleasure in them, and passing that pleasure on. To pass them on with any meaning we have to make them ours, to use them and enjoy them and show our children that we do, even if we only take them out of tissue once a year. The concept of home must be as of a beloved site if the possessions inside it are to do their work: possessions create a sense of haven, build memory, and cement relationships through the shared experience of caring for them. We have only to find new ways to tend each room.

Perhaps it's my having been steeped, as an anthropologist, in creation myths and totemic folklore, or maybe it was my childhood among the literatures of talking bestiaries, but I soon discovered the magical power of anthropomorphizing in homelife. I grant animation to everything. When my toddlers would bang into furniture, to distract them from their tears, I would stand, hands on hips, and scold the chair. "Don't you dare knock down my sweetie! Naughty chair, don't you know how to treat a little child? Now you sit down and stay out of the way." Sometimes the chair would sass back. Things that come alive bring a life of their own, as all Pygmalions know.

HOME AS TENT

Home as haven is something that starts when children beg to build tents in the living room. They are creating a sense of intimacy, enclosure, and safety, as they sit squat-legged under a sheet draped between pieces of furniture. This desire for envelopment is instinctual. In these small places of enclosure we are building our little nests; just like when you played in the back of the closet, the old and odd smells, dim light, the texture of the wood, the heavy drape of coat hems on your shoulder. C. S. Lewis made fine literature out of this feeling, in his *Chronicles of Narnia* series. He took seriously the adage that great writing comes out of the first havens of our child-hood. Vermeer also exemplified this experience in his interior paintings with their profound sense of stillness, that he captured, intimacy, and order. These elements must be present to make a haven. In their little cubbies, children are trying to set up house, to replicate a feeling and gain an understanding of what a home truly is. Once they get set up, everything they can imagine placed just so, they are ready to venture out. But first they replicate the concept of home in the same way that Solomon's temple was to be a reproduction of the real one up in heaven.

It seems the more we examine child's play, the more we discover how profound it is. To children, home is a playing field. The home children inhabit is different from the home you inhabit, even when it is the same one. They are living physically and literally at a different level than you are. Where their eyes fall, where their limbs touch and engage, are places we hover above and rarely visit. This means the memory world they are building is a separate one from yours, and as parents we need to take account of this. Children are always building a home within your home, no matter their age. Simple sensitivity to this fact can make an important difference for children, especially when we understand and acquiesce to such primitive behavior as tent building in the living room. In the frantic pace of modern life and the chaos of trying to maintain a home, let your children build a tent. Watch and see them make a place of serenity, envelopment, and order out of it. This is especially important because we cannot provide that for them each day. A magic bed is another version of this, attested to by the ever-popular canopied bed. In fact, some form of tent bed is a wonderful meeting ground for parents and children to inhabit at the closing of the day, even if you only stick your head in for that always vital nightly chat.

Teenage homes-within-homes are notoriously difficult to storm, and you may well question this notion of serenity, envelopment, and order as you stand at their door, but the same elements are in existence, even if you don't see them. They are still making sense out of their notion of home; and whatever it is that is in there is precious to them, even though it is currently lying under the bed.

Perhaps the most satisfying home-within-a-home is the one we have yet to realize, the one we anticipate by building up together experience, celebrations, textures, smells, familiar possessions.

HOME AND THE OUTSIDE WORLD

Home also has to be a haven from the great outside, a relief from the cacophony of the streets. Home has to be against the world, a place that resists intrusion. We create safety for one another out of this vital contrast. Indeed, the stronger we make this contrast, the stronger we send our children and ourselves out into the world. Homes cannot be a haven only, they must be more, even though they must be havens first. To create an interior domain, we must instill a sense of difference between the world and home—to create a demarcation, if you will, that home is counter to the world.

Homes as places of rest, nowadays, are in short supply. Why is this? For an affluent society, we work longer hours than hunter-gatherer tribes, whose labor anthropologists calculate averages around four hours a day. Though they have seasons of intensive labor, the rest of the time they spend socializing, cooking, relaxing, and preparing for feasts—the good life. It is a shock to realize how labor intensive our own society is. And how entrenched the work/home division is. We are no longer down on the farm, dropping our plows when the lunch bell is rung. Integration of home and workplace, though long gone, may be reemerging with the advent of the home office, but we're still a long way off.

Besides longer hours away from the respite of home, there is a more pressing reason why there are so few homes. There is no way to close off home from the rest of the world, no way to make that vital line of demarcation. The outside comes pouring in through the window of television, or the computer screen; it's carried in via shopping bags. Homes have always been used as retreats, but now we need them as shelters, not just from the elements, but from our own society.

THRESHOLDS

We are living in astonishing times, where the dissolute expresses itself everywhere, even right in the middle of our living rooms. No matter where you live—big city or small town—this porousness means you are living with urbanized, exposed children. The velocity children live at through the common media culture we share assures that. Even if they ride their bikes up the country lane they will come home to the television, the Walkman, the Internet. To establish our home as a haven, we have to do our gatekeeping seriously, with care and intelligence. When our children are young, we have to get up and turn off the radio when news of a rape comes on, and when they are older and that same news comes on, we have to sit down and explain what that means and what we think about it. We have to cry about it together, but we cannot, must not, let it pass unnoticed in our homes.

There are tricks to gatekeeping, to keeping the world at bay. The old tradition of carrying the bride over the threshold was a picture-perfect way of signifying a crossing, a transition—a symbolic expression that captured a reality. But that truth doesn't stop with newlyweds. We cross the threshold every day; we carry our children over the threshold too. It's a coming in. A threshold is like a compression chamber in which a deep-sea diver, arriving from the depths, decompresses into a native atmosphere. It is a place where the diver relishes what he's accomplished, but is glad to be back in the safety of the ship. The threshold is a locale where behavior and roles are changed from those worn in the outside world. There is, for instance, a father who cursed quite liberally outside his home, but never swore while inside.

We can mark our determination to gatekeep by marking our thresholds. Front door or garage door, mudroom or fancy foyer, mark your door. There is an ancient rule requiring Jews to nail mezuzahs, small boxes with scripture passages rolled up inside, to their lintels. This human instinct resurfaces on every college dorm floor—pictures, bulletin boards, flyers, lining hallway doors. Your door is a face to the world and presents a front for respect. We change the marks of our door depending on the life inside. Births, deaths, and passing seasons are announced over time. My husband started the tradition of posting obituaries of composers, writers, even municipal workers he loved and respected, on our front door, alerting those who entered that we mourned their loss. Of course, children's artwork appears too—why limit genius to the refrigerator door? Besides, those magnets never hold. Now neighborhood children come with their drawings, "Could this go on your door for a while?"

We build up our homes in many ways, through many different layers of meanings. Even thresholds have multiple purposes. While they serve as an entree to our havens, they are also openings to the world, the place from which we go out. Thresholds are a place of crossing, they go both ways—we are sending our children out to the world to influence it as well. This concept of threshold is ever shifting, you can't define it for long, and it will change as your children become older. It will become more porous. More will be able to pass in and out, and this cannot be changed. However, there must always be a sense of a threshold in your home—you must have a sense of passage, not only in, but out. Threshold doesn't require a formal foyer, it is conceptual and felt.

Not only people, but things, pass through the threshold as well, such as books, movies, toys—the culture from the outside world. But by coming over the portal, like the bride, these things begin new life in your home. Your home is its own society, and so when your adolescent brings a movie into your home, it must be seen through the eyes of the family, through the shared history that you have been creating as a family for years and years. It cannot be watched as it was watched by strangers in a theater. This threshold is how a family protects itself—because it must protect its interests against those of the world—but also it is how a family thrives, not getting stale and insular but responding to the artifacts and ideas of the world. The notion of a threshold works as a filter that allows children to take the things they've begun to acquire in the outside world and, in relative peace and security, begin to decipher those things.

I have often wondered why our culture makes such ugly toys. I don't have an answer yet, or maybe I just don't want to say it, but I did laugh when Luca was given a birthday gift and, after unwrapping it, looked at me and said, "Mom, I know you think this is too ugly to play with here, but do you think I could play with it outside?" "Fine," I snorted, disgusted at yet another dumb object in our life, but glad he made some distinction for himself.

LEADING CULTURE

Another powerful way to regulate culture is to give your children a crack at peer leadership. The most powerful tool to accomplish this is your home. Opening your home to peers places your children in the center and provides them with the possibility of making their home a place of excitement, action, interest, identity—which is what they are searching for from the outside world. This starts with tea parties for the four-year-old crowd, but can end up as the crash pad for your kid's high-school graduation party. Our neighbors host the all-star game for the neighborhood contingent of young boys. The amount of soda and snacks consumed is astonishing, but they leave satisfied with more than just their junk-food quota—they've been at someone's home, allowed to cut loose in a safe place, invited in, not sent out. An afternoon, or one night, of hell for you at your house, if it happens, is also a night of victory as a parent. You've kept your kids off the conceptual streets.

The streets are a metaphor for excitement even as they are a literal experience for some. They are the ultimate symbol for urban culture. The flashing movie marquees, the gritty back alleys, nightclubs, drug scenes, sirens, all clinically and calculatingly injected into our minds through media images, are so seductive because our homes are so dull. We mostly live in anonymous, look-alike houses, hermetically sealed, air conditioners humming day and night, carpeted from wall to wall, No Bugs Allowed. And from there we shuttle back and forth from our garage to our cars. We cannot, nor should we want to, make an impenetrable boundary between our home and the streets around us. Home should be a place where we filter, distill, and understand the world around us; our think tank.

We once had our little two-year-old in one of those carry backpacks, right before she kicked her way out of it. We went into a music store, which are now indoor streets, and were roaming around the aisles. We finally found what we were looking for, and as we stood, heads bent, calmly flipping through the jazz section, our daughter, up in the backpack, was locked on to a monitor hung from the store's ceiling, broadcasting a murder scene. No matter how much we monitor our children's incoming culture, there is no escape from the imagery of the streets, even if you live in a modest hillside town. Therefore, while we want to make our homes a haven, a sanctuary, we also have to make them more than just a rest from the world. They must serve as a place to discuss the world, to critique and assess. Homes need to be the seat of judgment, where we decide together what is good and bad, right or wrong, purposeful or lost. This doesn't mean we pack our home with action, but with meaning, relationships, conversation, rootedness.

That same two-year-old, years later gave proper dinner parties for her classmates at the end of the school year. She gets out "her" best dishes—orphan plates from good china sets, cloth napkins, place cards, a tablecloth. Decorating the table takes all morning. The centerpiece alone is a week's worth of ruminating. Wine bottles are placed on the table, filled with sparkling cider. Goblets, again mismatched finds, are set at each place, music is picked for the event, candles are lit. The children come, and appearing as dinner guests, they stand a little straighter when they ring the doorbell, before they make a dash for dining room. I only supervise the cooking. Mostly I hide out in the kitchen. Leaning against the door, I try to overhear the conversations. For the children, this event carries more weight than the latest film release, because they experience it as real. They are really coming to a formal dinner. We can offer the reality of our homes against the imagery of the metaphorical streets. We haven't lost one goblet yet.

What is it about goblets that gives me a lump right in the throat? To see a little fist brandishing one about, drink half-sloshing, ought to fill me with terror. Instead I get the deeply satisfying affirmation that, for the moment, we are princes of our palaces, little or big as we are. Goblets ring royalty bells for me, aristocracy, or even only mere martiniesque sophistication, but they symbolize elevation, reminiscent of a chalice. A goblet lifts you up, even as it lifts up the body of liquid you are drinking. The imagery of a child sipping from a goblet is a glimpse of a lost land, some original garden, where animals talk, flowers sing, feasting abounds, and every servant is a noble in disguise. Maybe our little diner parties for children are a silly attempt to taste this vision, but I can't give it up, even if we do, in the end, lose some goblets, in peril of a gash. When the other mothers come to collect their children, I know they contain their askance glances: I've let their children play with glass. I, too, wonder sometimes if I am a demented, too-casual mother. But I am not, I am crazy for the real. I so want to put the real into children's hands, to promise them while they are still children, still believers, that it is beautiful, exciting, and dangerous to be at a table.

And it's not just eating, but dining. Various cultures develop amazingly intricate rights to the family table. Just who gets to not only eat, but dine is an oft-battled-over issue. The table is the family altar. In human hands, the instinct toward food has been amplified beyond survival. It's gone right up the biosymbolic ladder to the top, coming out as concept, ideology, nay, theology! Food theology over daily bread, is precisely how we turn each other from mere bodies into kin. In dining across from each other we master the nature of our relationships. A seat at the table means you belong here. The table explicitly stands for family, for home—a family's identity, its games, its rituals, its cooking, are held, beheld, on the table. It's tribal. The whole idea of eating together is the right to call oneself a family.

Seven

Staying Married with Children

To Think a Marriage Sacred

*M*arriage is sacred, it is a living thing. It has its own life, a spirit, because all relationships are living, born just as a child is born out of any two coming together. No married couple is childless. The first fruit, or child, of matrimony is the marriage itself. We have to keep it, guard it, nurture it. What is born is bigger than the lives and desires of the two who come together. Being in a sacred state of marriage, which sounds perfectly comic because you've probably just finished swabbing the dinner dishes, means being moved closer to a vision, a transformation. Sacredness is always about becoming more. Hanging on to a sacred view of marriage holds us accountable for not settling for what we get, but always longing for more as a partner and from a partner. A marriage lived out under this awareness looks different—a long-cast perspective that lubricates us past the petty battles and buttresses us in for the long haul over the tough, rough issues that must be addressed if we are to make the marriage we want. You went through the ritual, The Wedding; now marriage is the time to think about the state that exact ritual initiated, indeed, injected you into.

Thinking of your marriage as a living entity moves you away from the most common, earthbound view of matrimony—a contract between two people who have come together to seek personal comfort and happiness. A contractual view emphasizes first the balance of needs of the individual parties, not the needs of the marriage itself. That never calls us any higher. And it deflates the rubbery raft on which both partners float in stormy seas. Into this raft, day by day, we each breathe trust; however, if you only exhale when your own needs are met, nothing beyond your own needs will develop.

Contracts come naturally to us; we are all lawyers at heart. We are surrounded by a contractual notion of marriage, a low view, and we will have a low-grade marriage unless we don't think in higher terms. To discover a vision of marriage is a call, a vocation; a marriage not muddled through, but made, created, claimed. Marriage that is thought of in this way is higher than us and calls us both upward. We think more about the future of our marriage and feel the urgency of doing something about it, breathing life into it, being willing to fight for it, instead of just surviving it.

SHARED VISION WITH A CLUNKER

Marriage is not romance, as endlessly advertised, but something far, far more primitive, born of our longing to be loved, to be held, to be seen, by one same person. What brings us together is a shared vision of a pledged life. We want to inspire and be inspired. In this way, marriage is different from all other relationships because we are privy to someone's deep desires for their future—and that is usually what we fall in love with: what we want to be in the future. In the meantime, we are and always will be married to the person of the present, who is not yet what he or she longs to be. This, too, is an important awareness to keep ourselves surrounded with, in the same way we think about sacredness, because it keeps us pulling forward, looking beyond the fleabites and doggieness of our spouses to our long-term goals of marriage, which was to be better to and for each other than when we started out. This is a very different vision than simply to learn to live together. To get someone closer to their future requires casting a compassionate eye on their past and to continue reading their life story in a compassionate way, with the hoped-for ending held in mind. Marriage is shared compassion on the pain of not being there yet.

MARRIAGE IS NOT FAMILY

Not being there yet, and longing for it, feels a lot like raising a family, too, but marriage and family are two different domains, double occupancy in the same sphere. It's vital not to mistake them for each other. This is why most marriages receive a shock when children come. Move over, something Really Big just arrived. We think we are still having a marriage, but we are having a family, from which a marriage has to be saved. There is room, however, for everybody, because love expands space, maybe even time, and I'd bet Einstein would concur. We are eternal creatures, really, infinite in our depths, capacities, thoughts, longings, soul, and so of course we feel a little jammed up between birth, death, and the length of the school day. Face it, now, you will never have enough time to do all the right things, the necessary, even important things you can eternally think up, but you will have enough love. Love somehow expands time. Not always, but I know that when I've taken the time to listen, it seems to work out even if we are late for school. I know when I've really sat down and listened, staying up to talk far too late into the night, or pulling over to the side of the road, even when late, the exchange seems to produce enough for the rest of the day. All else goes forward in the context of love, being loved, and giving. I guess it's the old loaves-and-fishes trick, plenitude out of limited resources. Maybe Jesus wasn't the only miracle worker. We are too. Family is a miracle. Marriage is a miracle. "Oh, yeah," we are conditioned to snort. "My marriage is a miracle! That's for sure—we haven't murdered each other yet!"

SORRY, WRONG NUMBER

You always marry the wrong person, the very person you end up wanting to murder, divorce, or lock in the freezer. It's a wonder that married people are even still alive, given that we only have a poolful of wrong, banged-up, sinking people to pick from. The fable that there is one right someone who'll save us from sinking is the longing for salvation love, just incorrectly aimed horizontally instead of vertically. Salvation never comes from the side, it can only come from above and beyond. We won't, as spouses, rescue one another, but we will float together, we won't suffer the dark waters alone.

A spouse becomes the wrong marriage partner right around the third month of marriage, just when you are in far enough to not be able to exit gracefully. Marta and Jack tell of the critical but still funny moment when Jack sat bolt upright in the dead of night, and yelled out, "LOVE you?!? I don't know if I even *like* you." Marta says she remembers the words appearing in her mind, in digital green, as if running like a news band atop a city building announcing headlines, *"STAY CALM, STAY CALM, STAY CALM."* Their photos from the honeymoon weren't even developed. Did they go on to have a midnight fight? Of course they did, and many others, but they fought within the facts that there wasn't somebody better out there who would be the One Who Really Appreciates them, that they had chosen each other to make something bigger than themselves, and that they had already been touched by the sacredness of marriage. Imagine a fight with those things out on the table. Marta, finally exhausted from fighting, rolled over in bed, and pulled up the covers and ventured cautiously, "Well, perhaps you'll like me by morning." A living marriage must make new trust, having bridged possible crisis. Making new trust: that makes the wrong person the right spouse. We have to keep making trust, too, night by night, anniversary by anniversary.

But trust often comes through crisis. A good marriage also need crises, many of them, from that first laborious year to the final funeral arrangements. A crisis is a chance to see someone and choose them, after the dirt is kicked in, and keep choosing them, over and over again, not just once. Crisis builds up existential trust, because finally finding yourselves on the other side of it binds you together. You wouldn't think of trading in that history.

We make trust not only with crisis, but with routine as well. After ten years of knowing my husband, I had one of those revelatory moments. He walked in from work, as he always does, distractedly taking off his coat, taking out his wallet, throwing it on the dresser, as he always does, he loosened his tie and took the change out of his pockets. While telling me about the day, he fished out all of the quarters, still chatting at me, and walked over and dumped them in a little can we keep on hand for the laundry machines. They pinged, and I stood there dumbfounded. In that gesture I knew he really was on board in our life together. It meant I didn't have to think of everything, we were working partners. Can it really be that mere quarters make marriage work? Yes, it is the small, almost oblivious, ways we assist each other that lay down layer after layer of trust. We are all Katharine Hepburn and Humphrey Bogart aboard the *African Queen*. And every day we are moving toward sinking or toward thrashing out to our destination.

DESTINATION: TRANSFORMATIONAL MYSTERY

What is the destination of marriage; is it companionship? Please, O God, let it not be a covert biological trick to make us reproduce ourselves as a diversified gene pool for the sake of species survival. That can't be it. It is not enough. But if we settle for being companionable, we can never be true companions in marriage. That's not enough either. We only need to read the four-thousand-year-old poetry of the Song of Solomon to be reminded of the universal aspiration for a partner. No, marriage is meant to transform us—transform us into something finer, better, richer, deeper, fuller. Far from being a generic, genetic conduit, my spouse is a secret Other, and only on occasion a familiar companion. In fact, we can never fully plumb the depths of mystery that we contain. We are always living with someone who has a hidden identity, each day revealing new riddles. Don't ever settle for the shallow truth that your partner's shown all. We arrive mysterious and we remain so. This mystery constitutes marriage. It's what we do with the mystery of each other that transforms us.

Life with a spouse is not unlike life with our children, a package that arrives, that we have to figure out, a little bit each day, who they are and what they want to become, holding on, all the time, to both. Our job is to help them be each, and don't forget to demand the same from them. I can't tell you how to do this, only that a sacred and anthropological view of marriage will help you look at things differently.

THE UNIVERSALITY OF MARRIAGE AND BEER

Of the few things anthropologists claim are found in every single culture are marriage and beer. Beer, well, more delicately put, fermented beverages. But nothing delicate can be said about marriage. It is a roaring affair, far outstripping beer in its induced passions, in its transformative powers. It is both sobering and joyous to discover that marriage is practiced and held sacred by every known culture.

To have perspective, imagine marriage in other cultures

and other times. What does a history of marriage tell? Or better yet, an anthropology of marriage? I can at least provide a synopsis, so you don't have to plow through the usual kind of ethnography—charting fief alliances and lineage strategies among the Maya, or infant betrothals to aged African chiefs—all the world's cultural tales that seem so quirky and make anthropology so interesting. It all points to sure evidence that everywhere people use beer to cope with living—and possibly marriage.

MARRIAGE AS GRAND ALLIANCE

The grand map shows that strategies of marriage are an attempt to get ahead, to create alliances. Anthropologist Claude Lévi-Strauss brilliantly envisioned the geometry of marriage in *The Elementary Structures of Kinship*, charting how women of a group are exported and imported in order to weave a society together through marriage. Alliance was the only way to survive. Indeed, whether in the grand mythological terms of Lévi-Strauss or in the search for someone to iron one's shirts, whether among the Dutch guild keepers or royal family alliances on every continent, marriage has always been seen as a chance to strengthen one's position through strategic partnerships. Contrary to the widespread practice called the bride-price, reading women as equivalent to cattle, Lévi-Strauss conceptualized the exchange of women as gifts. Before seeing women as pawns on a chessboard, raising our sisterly hackles, let us think a little further first. All men, all cultures, ultimately have to balance the overpowering potential of women to give birth. Patriarchy, it is speculated, was probably invented for this reason. It's an inadequate solution, and we can do better precisely by forming alliances of our own choice—that's the advantage of volitional marriage. Yet, in volitional marriage as we practice today, we are still looking for allies. We are still forming alliances in marriage; only instead of familial confederacies we choose personal allies to better reign over our private kingdoms. Now we are the kings and queens of our marriages. Say this to yourself frequently.

OUR MARRIAGE

Anthropology tells us two very important things about marriage and family: as mentioned, that they work as alliances, and secondly that they come in every form imaginable and still leave us with exactly the same work to be done: to be transformed. Emile Durkheim, an early father of social thinking, was mightily concerned with family and its place and influence in societies. His last great work was to be a broad treatise on this topic, but alas his final work was by death left undone. An acute social observer, Durkheim was concerned with rising divorce rates. Mind you, this was at the turn of the century when most of us think of family as having been in fine shape. It helps so very much to have historical and cultural perspectives when it comes to thinking about marriage and family. The proof of variation they provide unhooks us immediately from the "right" way to do it, the way It Is Supposed to Be Done, and frees us to consider how *I* want my marriage and family to be, putting us smack in the hot seat, the seat of responsibility, power, and passion—which is just where we should be, attached to our marriage, not some society's version of it.

Funny How Variation Ends up Looking Familiar

Even arranged alliances can—in fact, often do—have their own passionate attachments, perhaps even more replete with mystery. Look at the biblical story of Jacob and Rachel, for example. It's an interesting marriage story, not only to help us think about arranged marriages—for Jacob followed the pre-scribed marriage strategy, still widely practiced, of marrying his cross-cousin—but especially if we want to look at exam-ples of marriages with stepchildren, second wives, interfering in-laws, and throw in a concubine or two. These family histo-ries from the forefathers, complete with stepchild, half-children, adoptees, multiple marriages, substitute mothers and fathers, split-living arrangements, ecetera, aren't so very different from families today.

Jacob was wild about Rachel. He worked for her father for seven years to win her hand. But on the wedding night, Laban, her father, slipped her veiled sister Leah into the wed-ding tent. Jacob worked another seven years for Rachel and spent the rest of his life in the classic position of having married the wrong first wife and getting the younger one he wanted later, caught in the fallout between two households and rival children from each family. Does this sound familiar? In that culture, they didn't divorce, they just married again and again, but they had exactly the same emotional turmoil.

Frankly, the family has been in decline ever since Cain killed Abel, and we won't help ourselves by immortalizing any particular version of it—the chief thing is not determining and emulating the most successful version but being tenderhearted toward the people in your tent.

Thinking of marriage as an alliance is just another, more academic, way of saying that marriage is something bigger than just the two of you. Alliance brings strength and transformation. And alliances are for fighting the enemy. Sometimes we have to face the sad fact that our partner is the enemy of our marriage and bring that knowledge fully to light in order to go forward with an alliance.

Alliances are a boost, a hoist up to a new position, with new possibilities, new potentials. Marriage everywhere involves a serious status change, a new position marked by grand ritual. The door opens, you go from being one kind of person to another—you are initiated into a new role, that of wife or husband. Of course, you bring all of who you are to your new role, but you are not just adding on more by becoming a married person, you are being amalgamated, fused, into a new person. Here too, is transformation, begun in the ritual of the wedding. In fact, we really cannot be transformed alone, we need other people to become more than we are. In isolation, without new tasks to accomplish, without new roles to occupy, without a kingdom to create, we remain small, circumscribed. Of course, we do not categorically need marriage for this, with effort we can do this by our own single bootstraps, but marriage is the traditional route to transformation for a reason. It is the hottest furnace.

To Cleave in History

We can indeed draw a great deal from these histories to find companionship and solace in our own struggles. In fact, the very best marital advice is the oldest. It comes from Genesis' startling demand for marriage: *Therefore a man shall leave his father and mother and cleave to his wife, and they shall become one flesh.* Here again is the implication that marriage is to make a life beyond just each partner, they shall become one flesh, a new entity, something beyond each one alone.

I want to dwell on this expression of *cleave,* because inherent in this word is the profound longing behind what we are looking for when we talk about romance. Romance is just a snack when compared with the feast of cleaving. Cleaving is desperate, sexual, hot, exhausting. It involves a lot of yelling, demanding, yielding, sacrifice, fusion, vision, and letting go, leading unto union, and it implies fierce loyalty and ongoing affection. The *ongoing* is important. It doesn't mean cleave initially and then settle in comfortably for the long haul. Cleaving never loosens the clench.

The edict goes on, *and they shall become one flesh.* The original Hebrew does not imply oneness through having children—no children are as yet mentioned, but rather unity between two people, oneness forged out of two distinct types. Indeed, unity is an empty thought without two differing elements, two personalities first grappling to be together. This oneness doesn't come from the production of a third entity, as in children, but rather the experience of two facing each other. Children are the result, not the goal. The primacy of marriage over family shouldn't necessarily lead us to have childless partnerships, but rather to set the proper context for family, so our children may have a clear picture for their own adult lives and their future marriages. The first necessity of marriage is to cleave to our partners, each to the other, to make a life for each other, and invite children to orbit it.

My friend Anna told me, "When I had the baby, I didn't expect the competition my husband would feel for my attention. He was really scared because he had never seen me like that, so in love with another creature. I had to think hard about how to handle it, because I really did want to be with the baby more than with him. It was just that way, at least at first. I wouldn't even know he was in the room. But I saw he was scared and I felt sorry for him, so I started saying these little psych-up things, like 'Oh, honey, I think the baby's crying for you. You're the only one who can hold him like you do.' And you know what? It actually turned out that way, he would be the one person who could get him calmed in a certain way, and then I started thinking about us too. I'd say exactly the same thing, 'Oh, honey, you're the only one who can hold me like you do.' We got through it, but I think if I hadn't stepped back a little and made a place for him, we would have been pretty far down the road before I woke up and realized I had a baby and no husband."

We can extend this to say husband and wife leave their roles as mother and father and cleave to each other. I'm not suggesting you abandon the children, just don't abandon your lover. Get a baby-sitter.

Alliances also make room for new people, they enlarge the tent, though maybe not closet space. Unfortunately, in our society we see marriage as the one intimate relationship we are allowed. We ought to think about expanding our horizons a little. When we cleave to our partner, there's a lot more room for other kinds of closeness, of connection. Would that all our relationships were as rich as we could make them. Your marriage is the most important thing you will ever do. But you knew that—not Marriage, but your marriage, your partner and you in it. Maybe what you didn't know is that a marriage like that makes other relationships possible.

"When I married my husband, I knew I would get his family too," says Stephanie, first married at age forty-two. "Two daughters from a previous marriage and all the grandparents that came with that. I really thought twice, a couple of dozen times, about marrying him, but I kept thinking about being married, about making a life together, even knowing I was signing on for problems. In a way this was a good thing, because I already knew it was going to be tough, so when problems came, I wasn't hurt, I didn't take it personally, because I'd signed on for combat duty. Instead of looking just to him, or thinking about trying to pry him away from older obligations, I just kept thinking, 'We're in this marriage together, and I want to make something here.' Because everybody saw I had signed on for a lifetime project, I was accepted by other family members. Also, I kept reminding Ted that I was dealing with all this, you know, where are we going to spend so-and-so's birthday, my disciplining his daughters and being backed up, changing the way things had always been done—because I loved him and he better thank me for it. He treats me like royalty, and you know, it's kind of spilled over to everybody else. I thought I would just be stabilizing and coping with the fallout of being a second wife, but you know, I have really fallen for his daughters too. I didn't expect that."

CLEAVING FOR A LIFETIME

At the bakery where I stop off for my morning coffee, I recently watched a scene unfold. He was a man pushing sixty, patiently sitting alone at the table, hands folded, cap nicely tilted, quietly taking in the scene. I noticed him right away because he looked like he had a lot of life experience, and having become acquainted with a little of the local color, I knew he was long married to the café's baker, their children now all grown. His wife, a large woman wearing a long white apron, already worked over from the first batch of muffins, came out. I'd seen her many times, a worn, always smiling, matron. She came out from the very back where trays were steaming. She tiredly sat down opposite him and he brightened immediately. He reached across the table and tweaked her cheek. You could see his love for her, and her small resistances to it. He continued his pursuit, perhaps just to get a smile out of her—one just for him. He pushed his coffee cup toward her, offering a drink, and when she shook her head, he reached over and rubbed her shoulder. They exchanged a few quiet words, then she got up, her bulk shaking the table. He leaned forward, grabbing her hand. She escaped, turned, and dispensed a smile, heading back behind the counter. Thrilled, he kept his eyes on her, sipping her in, relishing her movements, her self, as he warmed his hands around his cup. "Now," I asked myself, "how did they sustain *that* through an obviously long marriage?" Of course, I didn't ask, but the word *cleave* came to mind.

Aspects of Transformation

We haven't yet explored fully the transformational power of marriage, hidden in mystery. The very person we cling to is a mystery, and just how much so will be discovered in the everyday living of all the inexplicable things they do—especially toward us. "How could you do that?" will be an oft-stated rejoinder in your conversations. Here's where we must have mercy toward that mysterious person, where we can be helpers who lift each other up as we stumble, fail, and collapse immobile in front of the TV. We are the Good Samaritan to our spouse, who is a stranger to us still. To be willing to care for, in practical ways, a person who is a mystery, and to give them the dignity of remaining a mystery, allows them the possibility of transformation. We close off when we predict how they will act; expecting the same old responses always seals a marriage's bleak fate.

There are several aspects to transformation. The first is the new role we've been initiated into, the new status or state we gain, the enlargement of our sphere, the addition of strength and fusion alliance brings when we become married. It is always valuable to recall and retell to each other your courting story, and remind each other of your wedding day. Your wedding ceremony is the picture on the cover of your marriage story, and it's good to recall details of this event.

The second aspect is getting pried out of being a single person. To stay married, especially when you have children, means you have to give up being single. "You're still acting single! You're on a TEAM now!" has been shouted at me, usually when I come home from the grocery store with the newspaper and a nice personal-size bag of chips, minus the milk and butter. Giving up being single in this day and age is equated with growing up, it means to stop being a child. But we can continue to find all sorts of ways to be a child in our marriages, even a hot-rodding teenager, if we want. Throw out any stodgy grown-up images of you in apron and spatula and tell him to keep his Hawaiian swim trunks. Some of the best moments in marriages are pretending *together* to be wildly single. We have some friends who, when they go out on a date, send the wife off to get ready beforehand at her old college roommate's apartment. That alone sets up a different atmosphere to the evening as he comes to pick her up. Lately, he's been bringing a corsage.

A third transformational aspect to marriage is the possibility of healing. Yes, marriage is meant to heal. It provides the opportunity to write a new edition of the story of the family you came from, with the ending you always wanted. We are all writing the stories of our lives, constantly reediting. The incredible power we hold in someone's life as their partner is to heal past hurts, to create with them new, living endings, to change their story that can seem so immutable. As we pass through the chapters of our marriage, first separating from father and mother, uniting, cleaving to each other, making children, changing each other, venturing out on our joint projects, and separating, in a different way, from our children, we write out new editions of our novels, holding out for the endings we envisioned for each other when first we met.

FROM LOVER TO PARENT

My husband and I went from being single, to married, to parents in ten months. Even if you take ten years to do it, the roller-coaster ride will travel the same wild tracks. As Bette Davis said in *All About Eve,* "It's going to be a bumpy night." Why is this? Shouldn't having children be the most forthright thing in the world? Sure, but not when having a baby plunges you into the depths of incompetency. We hardly know which end of a baby is up, though our professional capacities at work might be astonishing. We have to go to class to learn how to breathe for labor and delivery. But the classes only teach mechanics, they don't prepare you to be catapulted into a new relationship utterly unlike any you've had before. And not only that, but a relationship that definitively rearranges every other relationship you own, most especially with your chosen partner. And thank you, Dr. Freud, for further terrorizing us with the thought that we might trash our children. That's, of course, after we've tentatively decided it is not environmentally incorrect to add to the population.

Baby One was a surprise pregnancy. "How could I be expecting? I only just got married. What is this—the frontier?" Ha! *Expecting* is the most ironic word for it. I didn't have a clue about the power of the storm about to blow in. I remember the dark night, shortly after I'd mastered the cultured art of baby burping, when it came to me that I would have to teach this tiny breathing body every word in the English language. You can see from this that a new parent is ignorant, anxiety prone, and wildly exaggerative. What we need is a little calmly dispensed information.

The first thing that must be said to new parents is that it won't always be like this, we all promise! It is a season, indeed, a seasoning, to be a new parent. You will be an old parent shortly.

Jay Belsky and John Kelly, in their book *The Transition to Parenthood,* identify these important principles for surviving baby:

Surrender individual goals and needs and work together as a team. Here again, in sociological language, is the notion of creating an alliance.

Resolve differences about division of labor and work in a mutually satisfying manner. Start with sharing quarters for the laundry machines. If you have your own washing machine, discuss who will buy stain remover.

Handle stress in a way that does not overstress a partner or a marriage. Always remember you're fighting with the one you love.

Fight constructively and maintain a pool of common interests despite diverging priorities. You know to drop fighting with the myth that you missed out getting a better husband or wife and that you're working together on a sacred marriage.

Realize that however good a marriage becomes postbaby, it will not be . . . the same . . . as prebaby. That's right, you are transformed.

Maintain the ability to communicate in a way that continues to nurture the marriage. I still love you, I still choose you; and by the way, it's your turn to get up tonight.

Husband and Dad

What they don't tell you is the raw practicality you need immediately to manage these things. The smartest thing a wife can do for her marriage (and ultimately her family) is to hand off that new baby to her husband and get out of the house—no, not for half an hour. He needs a nice, long terrifying stretch of not knowing what to do. It's his equivalent of labor, and he's got to discover that he, too, can deliver. For your marriage, your baby has to become as soon as possible your joint project. To his credit, it was my husband who thought this up. "Honey, go away." He may have said this not for my sake, though, but for his. "But you don't know how to do anything," I said earnestly. "Well," he sniffed, "you were incompetent the day after the baby was born, too, remember?"

A husband needs to go quickly from thinking of this person as "The Baby" to raising his child Tommy, Bucky, or little Mary Kate. He can't do this unless Mommy gives it up, wrestles down the terror that the baby will surely die in his care, and be willing to live with resulting stains. What do you get in exchange for stains and your first terrified afternoon off? A modern partnership, it can come no other way. It takes an extraordinary man to be able to do this, and women can generate the transformation by handing over the reins. At this moment of transition it is women who have the power to make not just their parenthood, but their marriage as well. This cannot be emphasized enough, and if you need to call me for the percentage statistics of children who have died in father's care versus mother's care, I will provide them, but I won't relieve your terror here by printing them, because you should have the chance to find out on your own.

My husband tells the story—with grace, I might add—of the time he was stopped on a street corner, stroller packed for the day, with two kids under two. A kindly, doting, elderly woman praised him to the skies for being out with the kids, the bravery he exhibited taking on two babes, the thrill she felt seeing more men involved in child care. On and on she went about how beautifully he was caring for his children, all the while she was reaching into the stroller, surreptitiously wiping the children's noses, pulling their sweaters closed around their chests, adjusting their hats, refitting their mittens, and finally producing a snack from her bag. Here is the double social message that he was great but he hadn't done it, and thank God she had come along. Wife, sister, mother-in-law, or neighborhood lady, here is the real battle of the sexes. Few women really just let men care for the children, God forbid the mess! My poor husband couldn't cross the street without getting help, being reminded, however subtly, that he was playing at it valiantly, but could never really get the job done. To allow a man to become a father, and a fearless one, requires women to step back, to let go, to admit their own shortcomings. It makes for better mothers too.

It is hard for a husband to also be a father; equally, it is hard to be both wife and mother, this with just one body. You have to be very cagey, do it with all your mental prowess.

FROM WIFE TO ENDLESS WOMAN

I liked being a wife—for the few weeks I got to have it without anything else tugging on me—but I wasn't so sure I wanted to be a mom, although by delivery time, it was a little late to be pondering the question. I did ponder it, though. I suddenly had a lot of predawn philosophical hours on my hands, accompanied by rocking, rocking, rocking. I thought being a mom meant I now must sacrifice myself entirely for her sake, give up all my aspirations, put aside any thought of cultivating my own gifts, albeit keeping them as hobbies—as long as they didn't interfere with feedings. What new parents lack most is perspective. They have no idea how fast they are to be catapulted through these early stages. How can they have a perspective of speediness when the nights are endless? It seems apparent to everyone as soon as the baby arrives that this is it—right now is what parenting looks like, and it looks pretty bad. It is a terribly tender, fragile time, akin to sex for the first time. Your first experience at parenting will haunt you in the same way. But I had a philosophical breakthrough. Luckily I had a girl first, otherwise it might have taken me a few more years to work through to it.[1] Rocking, rocking, I

---

[1] Forgive the tangent, but I have often wondered about the differing routes into parenthood, either having a girl first or having a boy first. Random accounts I have collected tend to confirm the easier route for moms is the former. In part, I wonder if this reflects, as one mother stated, "With a girl I felt immediately in the driver's seat. I knew all about being a girl." Moms who have a boy first tend to talk about the strangeness of having a truly "other" little creature in their care and

kept thinking, "But if I am investing my total self in her so that she can take off and fly and reach her full potential, what happens when *she* becomes a mom, cut down in midflight, so to speak? It can't be that I am pouring myself into her so that she can turn around and sacrifice herself to her children. Hey, what about my mom—what does she want for me? Was she secretly raising me just to reproduce? Is there life for me past parenting? It *has* to be that I'm worth more than the moment I give birth and the rest of the time I'm downsized to slave." Oh, yes, parenting is slave labor, but only for the opening act, and it's a long, long play. Once I got a hold of the possibility that being a mom meant staying personally alive through all this, I got some relief from the voice, "It's Over. My life is Over," whimpering in my head.

In all fairness, I did say to my husband, "I think my life is over." "Nonsense," he said. "*My* life is over." But it was really *our* life that was over, as we knew it. It was a great life. They call it the transition to parenting, but I think it's really the great divide. It's like the boat to America. You look fondly back at the pictures of you in the old country. And you still have to stay married in this country. What happens to mothers is predictable: they will "do" the childcare. What happens to fathers is highly unpredictable and will chart the course of what your family will look like. If left to the predictable, fathers will continue, as they so often have, to lose out in the involvement, in the intimate knowing of their own children. And for the most part, this is what fathers have been shut out

---

especially the fear of unintentionally emasculating a son. These are, of course, just more thoughts to muse over in the rocking chair.

of. Fathers have been sent off to do the financial-responsibility stuff, when the best moments come precisely when you are parting your child's hair.

Men resist child rearing; women would resist a good part of it, too, except that would bring heaps of approbation down upon them. When men resist, they are considered, today, a little stuck in history's mud, but otherwise decent fellows.

There is a reason we all resist child rearing. Society tells us it isn't where the action is. Child rearing doesn't elicit the praise we get from other sources. There can be almost a sense of lonely shame as you "stroller" pass another parent. "Yeah, I'm stuck doing this too." You feel a little silly hunched over a dinky stroller. "See the birdie? It's a birdie. Birdie, birdie." And also—the secret is out!—child rearing can be one of the most boring tasks on the face of the earth. A friend who stayed home with his first girl said that, at times, the hours of his days passed as slowly as when he was forced by nuns to stay after school and write one hundred *I will nots* on the blackboard. Certainly sitting down and doing building blocks with a three-year-old *can* be one of the most exciting experiences a human can have. The flights of imagination, the glee in the eye, when ten blocks are stacked atop each other without falling, and petting a disappointed child when the structure topples over with the eleventh block, can move the human heart to new depths of joy and fulfillment—on Monday. By Thursday, the picture looks a little different. While your daughter piles the blocks up, you reach surreptitiously for the newspaper lying a few feet away. No matter that it's ten days old. You want to bust out of this world you inhabit from the time your partner leaves at 7:15 A.M. until arriving home at 6:30 P.M. Like an immigrant in a new land, you need a few things from the old country to remind you of who you are.

You *should* feel unnatural in this world. A normal adult can only listen to sing-along tapes for so long before the mind rebels at the repetition and simplicity. Women are trained to persevere through all this; men are taught to go outside and cut the grass. However, if truth be told, the man who is truly separated from the boys is the one willing to enter this world, endure and enjoy it, and help his children thrive. He must learn to make this world his own and move through it with some degree of fluidity; in that sense, he must be part owner of it. If he believes the diaper pail should go on the left side of the changing table rather than the right, for goodness sakes, let him do it. He needs to have a stake in this world.

Creating a Culture of Teamwork

To bring another partner into the teamwork of child rearing requires recasting the traditional goal of parenting: attending to the well-being of children. If that is the paramount goal, then you do whatever it takes to get the job done. This means that the less efficient partner is politely moved aside so the other can do what needs to be done: shopping, diapering, bathing.

Over the long term, this equation spawns an insidious anger, born of the resentment one partner feels at having to do the lion's share of work and constantly rescue the other.

The goal of the well-being of the children must be melded with another: Creating a culture of teamwork with your partner. As on any team, each member will have strengths and weaknesses. One partner might be a .300 hitter, the other a .230 hitter. But the weaker hitter must get his turn at bat without recriminations from the bench. Only if that team member is allowed to swing the bat will he get to be proficient. Now the goal becomes raising the children as well as possible, but also doing it together. And the joy is fuller for caretakers and the children as well.

If we lived in a different cultural context, we could draw on extended kin and baby care wouldn't fall so heavily on just two people. But we do not want to live with our mothers-in-law (pardon to all you *good* mothers-in-law). We do want to have a volitional marriage. Freedoms have their price.

FREEDOMS IN FAMILY

In fact, freedom is the ultimate issue in parenting, yours and the children's. You will spend the entire length of your family life seeking the balances of freedoms, from the stage where you feel hermetically sealed in with a newborn, tethered to a nurser, disciplining a toddler, to the freedoms you want to allow your teenager, the freedoms you give to your children to parent their own children, to the freedoms they provide as you age and can't drive anymore. There is astonishing symmetry in family life, which will find its best balance over the issue of freedom. Freedom is a lot like love, though. More generates more. As husband and wife, it is vital, especially with young children, to seek each other's freedom, to have mercy when your spouse has "that look." Hand your partner a twenty-dollar bill and push 'em out the door. For moms the balance of freedom is most often sought in getting beyond just child care, for most dads the balance of freedom that needs to be sought is true time caring for their children. Cagey freedom-giving within the confines of family life will always come back to bless you. "Yes, go," will elicit, "Hey, I'm home."

MOTHERS AND SONS

There are special qualities to being a parent to a child of the opposite sex, as Freud blasted into our consciousness. However, outside of an analyst's office, we don't much get to discuss raising a cross-sex child. What I'd like to note is not its trickiness, but its joys. A little boy in front of a big, powerful mommy is a tremendously fragile setting and when we navigate it well, with all of the delicacy, agile smarts, and supple grace it requires of us, it is womanhood at its shining finest. The work of mothering a son is mostly about stepping aside with precise timing. Think of bulls and bullfighting. It's not about going to the park and throwing a ball with your son, although that is a wonderful thing for a mother to do. We are the first face of romantic love to our children, a picture they go seeking. For moms it is trying to bring a boy into feminine culture to show how to be comfortable there too. To grow a son comfortable with and appreciative of the feminine is a cultivated and satisfying act and gives that son access to many mental domains. There is the thrill for women of raising a good man for a woman of the next generation. We know how valuable our product is! Okay, so we get a little opinionated—like about just who she will be—but it's only because we don't want the work to go to waste.

Sheryl, wife, writer, and English professor, and mother of two boys and two girls, describes growing a son as conferring a sense of independence within the mother/son context. "Now I take him with me to work two days a week and he sits there during my office hours while students come and go. Seeing me on my territory, he relates to me more in the sense of a mentor; there is a new kind of affection there. This, too, is conferring independence, but on me! He is seeing me in new ways, what a big 'girl' I am."

"When I take my son to work, the drive takes about a half hour. We are exploring together the history of jazz, and on the way there, we listen together to various jazz greats, but on the way home, we listen to his rap tapes and he tells me what he likes about them and I tell him what I like about jazz. It's a great trip. I was really touched recently when he found out there was to be a special morning radio show on jazz and he got up early and taped three hours of it and presented me with the tapes for our commute."

How is this different from how Sheryl is raising her daughters? "I want my sons, both of them, to learn from me that they are free to be rooted in home and still be abroad in the world as men." She also feels being a mother to her sons involves giving them pictures of her as a woman engaging her gifts. She is sharing her interests with them, preparing them to see women as partners, with many interests, giving them a model.

FATHERS AND DAUGHTERS

Social scientists have just begun to concertedly explore a father's role in a daughter's choice of partners. But little girls have known all along what researchers are only now turning their attention to: "Daddy, I want to marry a man like you." If the work of mothering a son is stepping back, the work of fathering a daughter is about stepping in. These are only metaphors, of course, never denying, but intertwined with, the ongoing daily presence and care of each parent.

A friend of mine once took his eight-year-old daughter to an upscale tearoom to celebrate nothing in particular. Well, yes, what the hell, they were celebrating life itself between a father and daughter. My friend didn't skimp or downplay the event in any way; he dressed to the nines. When he came to pick his daughter up at school, he had brought her her favorite dress to change into in the school bathroom. She left the school on his arm and off they went. Nature had provided an ice storm that afternoon, and so the trees glistened and crackled with a magical quality.

They entered the café and were escorted to a table. Like any gentleman worth his weight in salt, my friend helped his daughter off with her coat. When she went to grab a chair, he gently brushed her hand away and pulled the chair out for her. A few heads turned at the sight, and his daughter seemed to enjoy the attention, but was a little wary.

"Daddy, this looks very expensive," she whispered. This was truly a special treat for this cash-strapped family.

"Honey, have whatever you want," he said, knowing the

check would mean cold cheese sandwiches for him at work for the next two weeks.

The waitress, a middle-aged woman with a jaded eye that had probably seen the rise and fall of many relationships in this café, came over to take their order. My friend's daughter, envisioning chocolate raspberry cake with oodles of frosting swirls and a bottle of Coca-Cola with a lemon wedge, beamed like the Brooklyn Bridge on a crisp fall night.

"Well, well, is this a birthday?" asked the waitress.

"No," said the girl.

"Religious occasion?"

"No. We're just out for a special time."

A slight scowl faded from the brow of the waitress, and she looked down at the eight-year-old and said, "Honey, make sure they all treat you this way."

Fantasy? No. Chivalry? Yes. This eight-year-old may one day despise cafés with taffee-colored walls and whipped cream piled higher than Dolly Parton's hair. She may marry a biker and live in a tepee. But style isn't the issue here. My friend was creating a kind of template of anticipation and expectation. As for all girls, the first man of the universe for his daughter—her Adam, so to speak—is her father. It is through his life and comportment that she will judge and choose the men in her life. That afternoon, he was attempting to create a sense of the standard that she should expect from the men in her life, himself included. Putting relationships before work is a truth that not only daughters, but fathers also, need to experience. As George MacDonald, Victorian Scots father of nine daughters and credited as father of the fantasy novel, wrote and believed, *it is better to enter into the house of life than the house of fame.*

THE HOUSE OF CHILDHOOD

Parenting returns you to childhood. This time we do it with our own children in tow. This is one of the great and secret joys of parenting. Not only a return to your childhood, but the one you really wanted. You are in charge now and can write out the story line, the new endings to the chapters in your own childhood that hurt, using your childhood, your experiences, your judgments about what you longed for as a child, to enrich your own child's life and history. This is not the same as living vicariously through your child, not at all. Instead it's turning the struggles of your childhood to real use for your own child's sake. A guy who spends time with his kids because his father was never there (he well knows the ache of that absence) is reliving that hurt and yet salving it, transforming it by using his pain to his children's advantage. You may even find, after all these years, you are glad for the sufferings you experienced, when your child comes through the door with a tale you know well, and you can look them in the eye and say with true compassion, "I know how you feel."

MARRIAGE IN THE END

*A*fter all is said and done, your children will grow up and likely spend their daily life without you. But you will be in their thought life, for you will have imaginatively inspired it; in their memory life, for you will have richly stocked it; in their spiritual life, for you will always be their first hero. Yes, they will go away from you to make their own families. You will be left once again, as at the wedding, to face your spouse alone. This means you are among the lucky who made it through the whole family cycle. This image, of you as seasoned survivors together, can help you now, through the fights that taste like bitter herbs, the stony stretches of silence, the ache of loneliness in marriage. Holding the image that we will find our way together through it all, that we will craft the resolutions, is not a visual trick, but a serious, long-sighted consideration of possibilities.

IMAGINATION AND FAITH

When we idealize the family, we demonize it. . . . In order to live a satisfying life of soul, we need a rich experience of family, at home and in every aspect of life, but in order to fully appreciate the family in depth, we need a general intensification of soulful living. The only solution is to give increased attention to both of these needs, realizing that we could bring more soulfulness to our dealings with our own families, and that we could also turn to the family more frequently for our soul's need of security, guidance, relatedness, and tradition.

When I stumbled across this quote from Thomas Moore's *Care of the Soul,* I cried out, "Yes, but *how?*" How do I give increased attention to soulful living, when my children are out of clean underpants? This is where imagination came to my rescue. In many ways, this book is my lunge at the "how" question. It's the practice of imagination, and its resourceful application, that make my family life sustaining. Any family can be looked at for its version of chaos; we certainly feel its chaotic nature, but imagination allows us to both order and recognize the story of our own family.

Indeed, every family needs imagination, but imagination alone is not enough; it has to be coupled with faith. No family is likely to survive without faith. You have a spouse, a child, and those relationships have to be discovered as you, in faith, proceed. Okay, then, what is faith? I've found that a useful though temporary replacement for the word "faith" is "giving." Giving is the antidote to skepticism, cynicism, and depression.

The kind of giving we do toward our family when we won't be expecting a return is parallel to holding a dinner party. Life with kids, homework, and late-working husbands makes us say "A dinner party? You mean haul out all the china, polish the silver, find the candles, make the spectacular flambé dessert? You're kidding!"

My latest encounter with this is the story of a woman keeping me company while we followed our toddlers around the swings and slides. She regaled me with the horror of her first-in-five-years dinner party; how she shouted mercilessly at the kids all day to get out of her way, bludgeoned her husband because he forgot the wine, watched the vacuum cleaner explode in a cloud of dust minutes before the guests were to arrive, smelled the stove giving off a funny burnt-chocolate smell. You know what I noticed, when for a second I could glance away from our ricocheting kids? Her eyes were shining, she was shining. "Oh, God," she said, finishing her story, "it was a wonderful evening. No one left before two A.M., the kids fell asleep on the couch surrounded by adult laughter, my husband held court over a bottle of Armagnac. Do you know they drank the whole bottle I brought back ten years ago from France? I've still got a sink full, and I mean full, of dishes and burnt pans at home, but so what, I don't care. I'm back."

Twenty minutes later, without missing a beat, she asked me if my husband and I could get away for an evening at her house next month; she was planning a little dinner party. I went home thinking of the son who had painted eight extraordinary paintings for a rental house while his father took treatments at Mayo Clinic; the professor who buys a cake once a week to bring his aging mother; the couple who talks their way to the top of a building once a year; my mother and her pot with the arrows carefully drawn on by my father, aiding her even past his death. What had these families discovered? The beyond-the-call effort and energy each member had made inspired and consoled not only their own families, but gave more life to the giver.

Giving is faith. But faith is also receiving and we, too, need not only to feed, but be fed. I recently called to thank a friend for taking my kids for an afternoon. I thought it would be a brief and technical conversation about returning a coat she had loaned my underdressed daughter. (Boy, that had been a screamingly bad day with me featured as inadequate mother once again.) Instead, I caught her just as she really broke and I suddenly had a razor-smart, organized, slightly ironical and prickly but always generous woman weeping on my phone line. "Listen to me, young lady," I scolded. "Why do you think you can live your life and take care of your family

without being fed and renewed yourself? Get thee to a monas-
tery!"

We haltingly discussed what it would take for her to escape
for two days to a nearby retreat center (check your local list-
ing). Just going over the details of what would need to be
canceled or attended to if she were indeed to go astonished
me. You'll notice I have not recommended, like *Mademoiselle,*
Vogue, and *Harper's Bazaar,* to take a spa weekend. Mudpacks
are not going to do it. Faith is finding and building a slow
relationship with God, but where does our culture allow us to
do that, when does parenting allow us the time? I can only
remind you of what you already know, that you'll just be
caught in the material cycle, ever-spinning, unless you yourself break it and seek the silence where you will be fed at the
table of the Holy. There your spirit, and its best instrument—
the imagination—will be renewed.

One final thought about family, faith, and imagination.
Holding faith in one hand and imagination in the other allows us to stand, chin up, and face the remorse and guilt that
comes with all families. Profound regret, perhaps years of it,
paralyze us, but just on the other side is our family.

BIBLIOGRAPHIC READING LIST

Below are some of the books and articles that have helped me in writing *The Art of Family*. The scope of some is far more demanding than others—Vygotsky is hardly a man you want to lug to the beach. Nevertheless, each of these authors has helped me not only compose this book, but navigate my days.

CHAPTER ONE—CREATING A FAMILY THAT LASTS A LIFETIME
Goffman, Erving. *The Presentation of Self in Everyday Life.* Garden City, N.Y.: Doubleday, 1959.
Hareven, Tarmara, ed. *Aging and Generational Relations Over the Life Course: A Historical and Cross-Cultural Perspective.* Berlin: Walter de Gruyter, 1995.
Hochschild, Arlie. *The Second Shift.* New York: Viking Penguin, 1989.
Platt, Elizabeth Balliett. *Scenes from Day Care: How Teachers Teach and What Children Learn.* New York: Teachers College Press, 1991.
Ricoeur, Paul. *The Rule of Metaphor: Multidisciplinary Studies in the Creation of Meaning in Language.* Toronto: Toronto University Press, 1981.

CHAPTER TWO—THE MEANING OF PLAY
Huizinga, Johannes. *Homo Ludens, A Study of the Play Element in Culture.* New York: Harper, 1970.
Radin, Paul. *The Trickster.* New York: Schocken Books, 1972.
Smolen, Wendy. *Playing Together.* New York: Simon & Schuster, 1995.

CHAPTER THREE—FAMILY AND SPIRITUALITY
Berends, Polly Berrien. *Gently Lead.* New York: Harper Perennial, 1992.
Berger, Peter. *The Sacred Canopy, Elements of a Sociological Theory of Religion.* New York: Doubleday, 1967.
Coles, Robert. *The Spiritual Life of Children.* Boston: Houghton Mifflin, 1990.
Durkheim, Emile. *The Elementary Forms of Religious Life.* New York: Free Press, 1995.
Lowry, Lois. *The Giver.* New York: Bantam Doubleday Dell, 1993.
Moyers, Bill. *Talking About Genesis.* New York: Doubleday, 1996.
Otto, Rudolf. *The Idea of the Holy.* London: Oxford University Press, 1950.
Scarf, Maggie. *Intimate Worlds, How Families Thrive and Why They Fail.* New York: Ballantine Books, 1995.

CHAPTER FOUR—THE PHYSICAL LIFE OF FAMILY
Brown, Norman O. *Life Against Death.* New York: Vintage Books, 1959.
Gordon, Mary. "My Mother Is Speaking from the Desert." *The New York Times Sunday Magazine,* March 19, 1995.
Levinas, Emmanuel. *Time and the Other.* Pittsburgh: Duquesne University Press, 1987.
Whiting, Beatrice B., and Carolyn P. Edwards, *Children of Different Worlds.* Cambridge, Mass.: Harvard University Press, 1988.

CHAPTER FIVE—RITUAL IN FAMILY LIFE
Bynum, Caroline, ed. *Gender and Religion: On the Complexity of Symbols.* Boston: Beacon Press, 1986.
Douglas, Mary. *Purity and Danger: An Analysis of the Concepts of Pollution and Taboo.* New York: Ark Paperbacks, 1981.
Durkheim, Emile. *The Elementary Forms of the Religious Life.* New York: Free Press, 1965.
Lévi-Strauss, Claude. *Myth and Meaning.* New York: Schocken Books, 1979.
Mauss, Marcel. *The Gift: Forms and Functions of Exchange in Archaic Societies.* New York: Norton, 1967.
Turner, Victor. *The Ritual Process: Structure and Anti-Structure.* Ithaca, N.Y.: Cornell University Press, 1977.
Van Gennup, A. *The Rites of Passage.* Chicago: University of Chicago Press, 1960.

CHAPTER SIX—FAMILY AND HOME
Eliade, Mircea. *The Sacred and the Profane.* New York: Harcourt Brace Jovanovich, 1959.
Vygotsky, L.S. *Collected Works of L. S. Vygotsky.* New York: Plenum Press, 1987.

CHAPTER SEVEN—STAYING MARRIED WITH CHILDREN
Belsky, Jay, and John Kelly. *The Transition to Parenthood.* New York: Delacorte Press, 1994.
Giddens, Anthony. *The Transformation of Intimacy.* Cambridge: Polity Press, 1992.
Lévi-Strauss, Claude. *The Elementary Structures of Kinship.* New York: Beacon Press, 1969.
Mahony, Rhona. *Kidding Ourselves: Breadwinning, Babies, and Bargaining Power.* New York: Basic Books, 1995.
Segalen, Martine. *Historical Anthropology of the Family.* New York: Cambridge University Press, 1986.
Wallerstein, Judith, and Sandra Blakeslee. *The Good Marriage: How and Why Love Lasts.* New York: Houghton Mifflin, 1995.